In the
Shaker
Tradition

In the Shaker Tradition

Lesley Duvall
Sharon Duane Koomler

FRIEDMAN/FAIRFAX

A FRIEDMAN/FAIRFAX BOOK

© 2002 by Michael Friedman Publishing Group, Inc.

Library of Congress Cataloging-in-Publication Data available upon request.

ISBN 1-58663-137-3

Editor: Susan Lauazu
Art Director: Jeff Batzli
Designer: Kevin Baier
Photography Editor: Paquita Bass
Production Manager: Richela Fabian Morgan

Color separations by Bright Arts Graphics, PTE, LTD
Printed in Singpore by CS Graphics, PTE, LTD

1 3 5 7 9 10 8 6 4 2

Distributed by Sterling Publishing Company, Inc.
387 Park Avenue South
New York, NY 10016
Distributed in Canada by Sterling Publishing
Canadian Manda Group
One Atlantic Avenue, Suite 105
Toronto, Ontario, Canada M6K 3E7
Distributed in Australia by
Capricorn Link (Australia) Pty, Ltd.
P.O. Box 704, Windsor, NSW 2756 Australia

Put your hands to work and your hearts to God.
Mother Ann Lee

◉ CONTENTS ◉

THE SPIRIT OF SHAKER

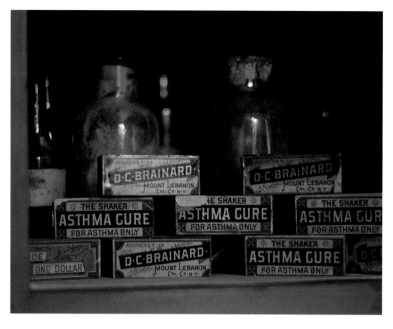

PAGE 8: Shaker settings, with their focus on simplicity and their pleasing symmetry, invoke an air of serenity. This elegant wash-stand, with its slightly flaring curly maple splashboards, would have been shared by the four residents of the room.

ABOVE RIGHT: At the height of "modern medicine" in the nine-teenth century, Shakers participated in the growing pharmaceutical industry. Known for quality products and honest business dealings, they marketed a wide variety of goods to the World. These colorful "Asthma Cure" packages originated from New Lebanon in New York.

OPPOSITE: Just as Shakers mixed furnishings that showed influences from the World with their own exquisite pieces, so, too, can today's home decorator. The timeless design of Shaker side chairs complements the fine-ly crafted spiral staircase in this entry hall.

For most of us, the word *Shaker* conjures visions of well-crafted rocking chairs, sweetly shaped oval boxes, and high-quality seeds and herbs. We think of the style as simple and clean-lined, and often apply the Shaker label to any number of pieces that share this aesthetic. Commonly for sale today are furnishings—including computer desks and bar stools—that no Shaker produced or designed, yet these pieces are identified as Shaker. Appropriating the Shaker name was, in fact, a practice that occurred even while the Shaker community was still vigorous, as an 1884 lawsuit attests. The beauty, fine craftsmanship, and/or efficacy of Shaker products—from chairs to health tonics to farm produce—was well established by the middle of the nine-teenth century, along with the Believers' reputation for honesty and fair dealing, and other manufacturers were inclined to trade on consumers' respect for Shaker goods.

It is a testament to the quality of the Shakers' designs that their furnishings and acces-sories are today not only sought after by collectors but are widely reproduced and used as models for countless furnishings and accessories that have been inspired by Shaker works. And while purists may object to reproductions or especially to furnishings more liberally adapted from Shaker designs, these pieces have certain virtues for home decorators who admire the aesthetic but are not ready to commit to collecting authentic vintage pieces.

One challenge of decorating a home with authentic Shaker furnishings and accessories is the cost involved. While the pieces have always been valued by collectors, since the 1980s the price of Shaker works has been rising steadily, sometimes making dramatic leaps, and several

thousand dollars for a small oval box is not unheard of. Documented, authentic pieces are rapidly vanishing from the marketplace, making it even more difficult to collect genuine Shaker articles. Perhaps more realistic for all but the wealthiest and most dedicated of collectors is the practice of acquiring a mix of cherished antiques, faithful reproductions, and pieces that take inspiration from the Shaker aesthetic.

In addition to being more affordable, reproductions and pieces that borrow from Shaker design styles have the virtue of being easy to live with. Homeowners, particularly those whose families include children or pets, can relax with their furnishings without worrying about breaking the pieces or marring their finishes.

It's also most likely that home decorators will mix their Shaker-style acquisitions with furnishings and backdrops of other styles, for few modern families would happily live in a collection of truly authentic Shaker rooms. Based on religious tenets and the practicalities of communal living rather than the comforts and needs of today's families, the arrangement and furnishings of Shaker rooms are spare and severe given our modern sensibilities. Rather, most will prefer to incorporate select Shaker pieces into rooms with a more eclectic style or to adopt an overall impression of simplicity while infusing the space with the warmth of personal possessions.

One practical effect of blending Shaker items with furniture of other decorative styles is increased comfort. Cozy upholstered sofas and armchairs allow a level of relaxation absent in the vocabulary of Shaker furniture, which was made exclusively of wood except for some chair seats. Today, we wouldn't dream of decorating a living

RIGHT: A classic Shaker-style rocker and a side table that borrows from the Shaker aesthetic are perfectly at home in this eclectically furnished log cabin. The pieces mix comfortably with a Victorian-influenced chair and drop-front desk, as well as with the wall-to-wall carpeting and white walls.

OPPOSITE: Many pieces of country furniture are attributed to Shaker craftsmen—the beautiful, functional designs of both Shaker and American country pieces appeal to our nostalgic sense of simpler lifestyles. In fact, many Shaker designs are based on the basic, familiar vernacular forms of early American furnishings.

ABOVE RIGHT: This Colonial-inspired dining room provides a perfect example of the forms from which Shaker craftsmen drew influence. Shakers took the traditional ladder-back chair, refined its form, and marketed it to the World.

room without comfortable seating areas where family and friends can gather or where we can settle in with the newspaper or a good book. But Shaker furnishings and accessories also have their place in such settings; they contribute crisp lines and an air of simplicity, as well as an appealing sense of the past. A stack of oval wooden boxes placed on an end table showcases a legacy of fine craftsmanship and graceful design combined with functionality, while a set of tape-seat ladder-back chairs adds warmth to a dining room with a sleek, modern design.

In fact, Shaker pieces' ability to blend into a variety of décors is perhaps their most appealing trait. Shaker furnishings are at home in rooms with a country flair or those that adopt a colonial design, and in fact their forms are largely drawn from vernacular designs common in the colonial era. But Shaker furniture and accents are equally well suited to contemporary settings where industrial materials and streamlined forms prevail. Because Shaker pieces are constructed of natural materials, they lend warmth to contemporary rooms and

provide a link with tradition, yet their clean lines and functionality carry a prescience of modernity, which keeps them in character with their twenty-first-century setting. These versatile pieces also fit well into eclectic rooms that combine styles across continents and centuries. In these mixed and often eccentric settings, Shaker furnishings offer a vital link between past and present, tradition and innovation, practicality and elegance.

And decorators need not invest in entire suites of Shaker-style furniture to imbue their homes with the signature aesthetic. Simply editing a room down to its essential elements and using a single Shaker chair, washstand, or other piece as focal point recalls the philosophy of Shaker design. A small collection of Shaker accessories may be all that a room needs to lend it warmth and character: oval boxes, tin sconces or candleholders, vintage sewing notions, or even framed graphics such as seed packets or jar labels can all infuse a space with an earnest Shaker quality.

In the Shaker Tradition honors the material culture of the Shakers with photographs of authentic Shaker settings and furnishings together with faithful reproductions, but it also celebrates the legacy of the Shakers by considering the way people interpret Shaker style today. In the pages of this book, readers will find inspiration for imbuing their own homes with the Shaker spirit, as well as a greater understanding of the philosophies and religious beliefs that informed Shaker lifeways, and thus their graceful yet pragmatic architecture, furnishings, and household objects.

ABOVE RIGHT: This room and the objects in it, exhibited at Hancock Shaker Village, could just as easily be found in a contemporary home. Brother Isaac Newton Young's quintessential wall clock hung in dwellings, shops, and barns, and today is widely reproduced.

OPPOSITE: Paring belongings down to the essentials, furnishing living spaces with clean-lined pieces like these Shaker-style backed benches and a drop-leaf table, and enhancing the sense of light and air in your rooms are all excellent ways to emphasize a Shaker aesthetic in your own home.

Chapter One

THE SHAKERS
Traditions and Folklife

In May of 1774, the charismatic religious leader known as Mother Ann Lee (1736–1784) set out from Liverpool for the New World with eight followers, including her husband, Abraham Stanley, and her brother William. An illiterate textile worker who grew up in poverty in the Manchester slums, Ann Lee perhaps seems an unlikely choice to head a church, but she was a powerful and persuasive speaker whose strong religious convictions and unshakable faith drew devoted followers to her.

Though little is known of Ann's early life, and she left no journals or letters as she could neither read nor write, by all accounts her family were religious Protestants. Sometime around 1760, Ann joined a group of religious extremists called the Wardley Society, founded by James and Jane Wardley. This group sought to free Protestantism from its unseemly excesses, taking inspiration from the Camisards, French Calvinists who had immigrated to England to escape persecution by the ruling Catholics in their homeland. Among the practices that members of the Wardley Society adopted from these dissident French Protestants was a manner of worship that included the "mighty shakes," brought on when worshipers were infused with the power of the Holy Spirit. Because of this violent trembling and the whirling dances performed during services, the group came to be known first as "Shaking Quakers" and later simply as "Shakers."

The force of Ann's personality and the strength of her faith raised her stature in the eyes of the other Shakers, and they came to rely on her leadership. They considered her a spiritual

PAGE 18: Classic Shaker pieces, including a painted round box and a straw hat, create a peaceful vignette in this room at Hancock Shaker Village. Wide windows and built-in drawers are other hallmarks of Shaker interior architecture evident in this setting.

ABOVE RIGHT: In nineteenth-century Shaker villages, significant buildings that faced the main road were often fronted with a white picket fence. This fence, in front of the Meetinghouse and Ministry Shop at Sabbathday Lake, is topped with unique flame-shaped points.

"parent," and began calling her Mother Ann. Like Christ before her, she brought God's word and the promise of salvation to all humanity.

She also received visions from God, and in one of these moments of revelation she understood the main cause of human suffering to be our sexual impulses and the resulting strife between men and women. She had suffered the loss of four infant children, and may have believed this was a punishment for her carnal activities. From this point on, Mother Ann preached a resolute celibacy for the members of her group.

Despite persecution and repeated arrests in England for heresy, she continued her preaching. It was during one of these periods of imprisonment that Mother Ann became convinced that God meant her to lead her people to America, where an untold number of

RIGHT: This engraving by non-Shaker Joseph Becker, published in 1873, gave the world his impression of the Shakers' worship service. Shakers were given that name by non-Shakers because of the ecstatic dance that was part of their worship.

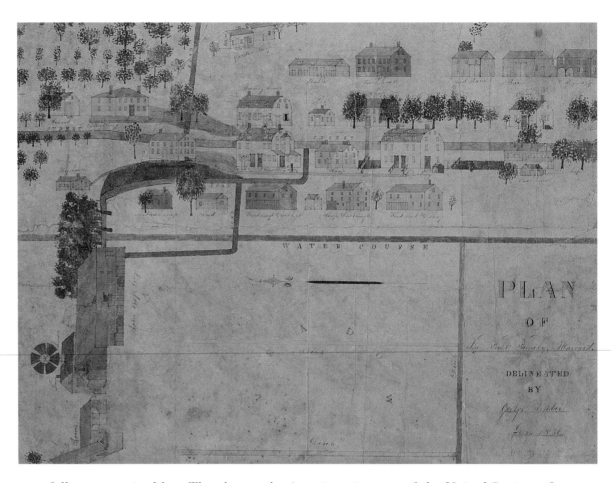

new followers awaited her. Thus began the American journey of the United Society of Believers in Christ's Second Appearing, as the Shakers officially named themselves.

A New Beginning in America

The road in America was not to be a smooth one for Mother Ann and her disciples. Troubled at their arrival by a lack of money, the Shakers were forced to separate in order to support themselves. During this time, Ann's husband left her and she worked long hours as a washerwoman, but she persevered in her belief that she would succeed as a missionary in the New World.

More than a year after their arrival at the port of New York, the group settled at Watervliet (also known as Niskeyuna), near Albany, New York. Difficult times continued for the Shakers, however, as Mother Ann's vision of a new ministry filled with Believers was slow

ABOVE RIGHT: Shakers documented their villages with elaborate maps. These drawings included more than just roads and property lines, they also featured buildings, gardens, orchards, and even animals and people.

OPPOSITE: Floors in shops and dwellings were frequently stained yellow, while walls were plastered or painted white. Interior trims varied from village to village, and from era to era. The paint in the Ministry Shop at Sabbathday Lake, shown here, reflects the building's nineteenth-century finishes.

to materialize. All that was to change when she won as a convert the Reverend Joseph Meacham, a Baptist preacher who brought much of his flock with him. The addition of Joseph Meacham and his congregants to the small Shaker community represented a sig-

nificant step for Mother Ann's mission. She knew, however, that to gain a wider audience for her message and find additional Believers she would have to leave her haven in the Hudson Valley and travel through the fledgling country. The period after the American Revolution was a time of religious zeal in the new nation—Americans were looking for assurance that they were in God's favor, and Mother Ann spoke convincingly of a way of life that invited God's grace. In 1781 she undertook a missionary tour, together with her brother William and a trusted follower, James Whittaker.

Mother Ann preached the virtues of honesty, humility, charity, and simplicity, all very much in keeping with other Christian teachings of the time. But she also embraced complete celibacy and equality among all people, ideas that not only deviated from accepted custom but were contrary to the law. Mother Ann's belief in the dual nature of God—that God encompassed the feminine as well as the masculine—was viewed as heresy by eighteenth-century Americans, and in fact would be seen as heretical by many people today.

After two years of her ministry tour, during which the group traveled through New York, Massachusetts, Connecticut, and Rhode Island, Mother Ann and her companions returned exhausted to Watervliet. And while they had attracted many new converts, they had also awakened the type of harsh judgment and persecution they had fled in England. Just one year

OPPOSITE: Paints were a common finish for wood in the eighteenth and nineteenth centuries, as they both preserved the wood and added visual interest. Shakers made use of paints in a manner similar to their neighbors.

ABOVE RIGHT: One of the many improvements made by Shakers to domestic tools is the double rolling pin. This device makes rolling out dough a breeze—the double action keeps the dough flat, preventing it from rolling up off the surface.

LEFT: Agriculture was at the core of Shaker industry. Shakers were progressive farmers, as evidenced here by the use of silos at the 1826 Round Stone Barn at Hancock.

after their return William died, and a little more than a month later—drained by her ministry tour and distraught by the loss of her beloved brother—Ann followed him to the grave. Mother Ann had lived in her promised land for a decade, and in that time had established a church that would take root and flower, becoming the most vigorous communal society ever to flourish in America.

LIFE IN SHAKER SOCIETY

Though Mother Ann had laid firm foundations for what would become a faith that included a belief in the equality of all people, no matter their race, gender, or family background; a commitment to celibacy; separation from the World; and community ownership of property, she died before the founding of the communal villages for which the Shakers are so well known. Upon the death of Mother Ann, the leadership of the Shakers was left in the capable, if uninspired, hands of devotee James Whittaker, who died just three years later.

Joseph Meacham, the Baptist minister who had been one of Mother Ann's first American converts, and Lucy Wright, an energetic and devout young woman, then became the spiritual leaders of the Shaker community. Father Joseph and Mother Lucy, as they were respectfully known, shared a strong vision for a society that was united not only in their religious beliefs but also in a collective desire to act out this union in their daily lives. Believers would come together to live, sharing all their property and worldly goods, as well as their labor and talents. In this way they could express both their unity as a people and their union with God. The Shakers built a meetinghouse at New Lebanon, New York, and there, at Christmastime in 1787, a group of about one hundred began their lives together.

Through the end of the eighteenth century and well into the nineteenth, the Shaker movement grew and new communities were established in Massachusetts, New York, New Hampshire, Maine, Connecticut, and eventually in Ohio, Kentucky, and Indiana, with all of these modeling their settlements after the one at New Lebanon. Church teachings stressed union of belief, and this emphasis

OPPOSITE: This interior, at South Union's Center Family Dwelling, shows the dual entries into the meeting room and the railings of the twin staircases that allow the segregated passage of Shaker Brothers and Sisters. The arch is an elegant but effective structural support for an interior weight-bearing wall.

on union was carried through every aspect of life: layout of the villages; architecture of meeting-houses, dwellings, and outbuildings; social structure; and the design of furniture, implements, and household goods were intentionally and strikingly similar from community to community, allowing for some influence from regional styles and traditions.

Over time, the organization of Shaker communal life evolved into a system that satisfied the Believers' wish to live out their faith in their daily lives and addressed as well the practical needs of large groups of people living together. It also represented what was perhaps the most egalitarian society in America to date.

All Shaker communities were organized into "families," in which Believers were grouped according to their commitment to the faith. Senior members, who had signed a pledge of faith known as the Covenant, were typically part of the Church Family, usually the largest and

best-established of the orders. Depending upon the size of the community, there were also a number of other families, named for their orientation to the Church Family—for instance, the North Family, South Family, and so on. Occasionally other names, such as Center Family in place of Church Family, or Second Family (for its chronological rather than geographical position) or Hill Family (for a feature of the landscape) were part of family nomenclature. These secondary families were sometimes overflow from the Church Family, created when the family became excessively large, but could also be composed of junior members or of novitiates, new members who had not yet relinquished their property and personal possessions to the group.

The Shakers desired converts and welcomed new members wholeheartedly, but realized that the decision to separate from the World, as they characterized the lands and peoples beyond their villages, was not one to be made lightly. They had also learned that, in times of hardship, followers were sometimes attracted to the church because of the relative security that life in a Shaker community offered. These followers were often called "winter Shakers" because they arrived at a time of year when work in the Shaker village was relatively light and food in their own households was scarce. When conditions in the outside world improved, these temporary converts left the church.

Each family had its own dwelling, workshops, barns, and outbuildings, and constituted a small neighborhood within the larger Shaker community. A system of governance within families was installed as well, with each family relying on well-respected men and women to see to

ABOVE RIGHT: Shakers are credited with a number of inventions that were adopted by the World. The flat broom—bundles of broom corn that were flattened and sewn into shape—allowed the more efficient and thorough cleaning of dwellings, shops, and barns. Broom making was a major industry for many Shaker villages.

ABOVE: An illustration from *The Shaker Almanac*, published by A.J. White, shows Shaker Sisters filling orders for medicines.

SHAKER COMMUNITIES

Watervliet (Niskeyuna), New York: 1787–1938

New Lebanon (Mount Lebanon), New York: 1787–1947

Hancock, Massachusetts: 1790–1960

Enfield, Connecticut: c. 1790–1917

Canterbury, New Hampshire: 1792–1992

Tyringham, Massachusetts: 1792–1875

Alfred, Maine: 1793–1931

Enfield, New Hampshire: 1793–1932

Harvard, Massachusetts: 1791–1918

Shirley, Massachusetts: 1793–1908

Sabbathday Lake (New Gloucester), Maine: 1794–present

Watervliet (Dayton/Beulah), Ohio: 1806–1900

Pleasant Hill, Kentucky: 1805–1910

South Union, Kentucky: c. 1807–1922

West Union (Busro), Indiana: c. 1807–1827

North Union (Cleveland), Ohio: 1822–1889

Whitewater, Ohio: c. 1826–1916

Sodus Bay, New York: 1826–1836

Groveland, New York: 1836–1892

In addition to the established communities listed here, there were also several short-lived Shaker communities and missions:

White Oak, Georgia: 1898–1902

Narcoosee, Florida: 1895–1924

Philadelphia, Pennsylvania: 1858–1896

the overall welfare of the group. Elders and Eldresses were responsible for their charges' spiritual well-being. Trustees, both male and female, handled finances and dealings with the World, while Deacons and Deaconesses supervised the various departments of labor, such as the kitchen, farm, shop, and laundry.

Children lived separately, cared for by two adult Shakers—men looked after the boys and women after the girls. Boys often lived in the upper floors above the Boys' Shops and girls in the floors above the Girls' Shops. Children were allowed to be children, and were usually removed from adult activities so they were not a distraction. Shakers believed in education for their young people, and provided the same curriculum to both boys and girls, though each gender attended school at a different time of year—girls for three months in summer, when the boys were busy with outdoor chores, and boys for three months in the winter. These schools gained such a reputation for excellence that, when the Shakers opened their classrooms to nonbelievers, many sent their children to be educated there.

Children came to Shaker villages in several ways. New converts often brought their entire families with them, and Shakers took in orphans and children whose parents could no longer care for them. Young people raised by the Shakers were free to choose their own beliefs when they reached adulthood, and many left the Shakers to rejoin the World, though some stayed, committing their lives to Shakerism.

Unlike other utopian groups that aspired to a life of celibacy, the Shakers did not segregate their members by gender. Men and women lived together in the same dwelling, though they occupied different sides of the building and typically used separate entrances. Labor was gender-specific in the Brethren's and Sisters' Shops.

To build solidarity and prevent resentments, Shakers held nearly all their possessions in common. Work, too, was shared, and each person was expected to contribute what he or she was able. The Elders and Eldresses who oversaw each Family and the Deacons and Deaconesses who were responsible for daily details such as scheduling devoted much effort to making certain that tasks were

OPPOSITE: Shakers were not encouraged to write, however Trustees, who managed the Believers' worldly affairs, were required to keep accounts and other records. This Maine Shaker desk reflects the changing tastes of the Victorian era in its more ornamental look. Shaker craftsmen refined the office chair, creating a low-backed revolving chair that was often used in front of a desk.

SHAKER APPLE SAUCE

Address **D. C. BRAINARD,** MT. LEBANON, COL., CO., N. Y.

apportioned fairly, with no one individual burdened with too much of the heavy work. Though Shakers believed in the equality of men and women, they divided their labor along traditional gender lines, with men doing most of the farming, carpentry, smithwork, and such, and the women performing tasks like cleaning, cooking, laundry, spinning, and sewing.

As the sect grew and life became more complex, Shaker leaders saw the need for a formal set of rules to live by. In 1821, the Millennial Laws were written to codify the behavior of the Shakers and the details of their daily lives, right down to appropriate paint colors for various buildings, the right fabrics for curtains, and the proper dimensions of mirrors. Over the years, the Millennial Laws would be revised several times to keep pace with the changing world and to define for the Shakers their place within it.

By the 1840s, Shakerism had reached its pinnacle, with as many as five thousand people living in nineteen communities. But a movement that required such sacrifice from its members was difficult to sustain, and, by 1875, the first well-established settlement to close, Tyringham, Massachusetts, had shut its doors.

The period of religious fervor that had infected the country passed with the Civil War, and the fresh availability of good farmland in the West drew away those who might have joined the Shakers for security. In addition, new institutions provided for the care of widows, orphans, and neglected children, leaving the Shakers bereft of another source of new members. From 1875 on, settlement after settlement was forced to disband, and today only Sabbathday Lake in Maine houses an active Shaker community, though several of the other villages have been restored and now function as living history museums (see Resources)

ABOVE RIGHT: Attractive, colorful labels helped effectively market many high-quality Shaker products. Thousands of gallons of applesauce were sold from the New Lebanon Shaker community in New York under the direction of Trustee D.C. Brainard.

OPPOSITE: The back hall in Hancock's 1830 Brick Dwelling is visually divided by a bell rope that runs through several stories. The bell was a great communication tool, used to call members in from shops and fields for meals, meetings, and emergencies.

Chapter Two

TOWN AND COUNTRY
*Shaker Architecture
and Landscapes*

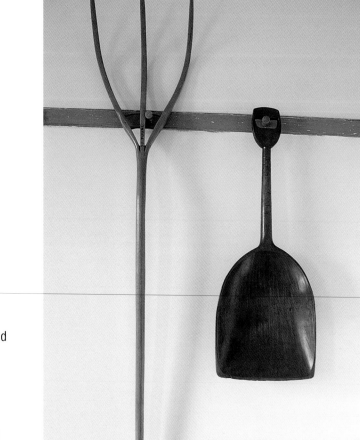

PAGE 36: Order is apparent in every aspect of Shaker architecture and landscape. At Sabbathday Lake, the perfectly symmetrical and beautifully proportioned meetinghouse, viewed from its side, and the adjacent garden, which is planted in careful rows, are evidence of the Shaker passion for balance and organization.

RIGHT: Many of the tools used every day in Shaker villages may be considered sculptural works of art. The symmetry and balance that make the tools beautiful to behold also render them more efficient in the hands of the user.

OPPOSITE: Clapboard buildings of simple but careful construction were abundant in all of the Shaker communities. Even secondary buildings, such as the 1833 Water House and the 1860 Brethren's Bath House at Pleasant Hill, benefited from scrupulous attention to detail, and contributed to the neat appearance of Shaker villages.

In a heavenly marriage of form and function, Shaker architecture reflected the tenet that Believers should strive for perfection in everything they built, for even their labor was a way of honoring God. The buildings' simple lines and unadorned forms, as well as the Shakers' exquisite craftsmanship, helped define the sect's architecture. But Shaker architectural forms also drew heavily upon local building traditions and the resources of the region.

The earliest Shaker settlements were located in New York and New England, areas that were dominated by English architectural styles modified to suit the availability of materials and the dictates of the climate. Shaker villages typically grew up around existing homes of early converts, and the architecture evolved as new buildings were constructed to suit the Shakers' communal way of life. Clapboard and brick buildings of Federal or Georgian design were common and, if not for the scale of Shaker architecture—which was grand—and the separate entrances for men and women, many of the Believers' early buildings would have been barely distinguishable from others of the period.

Shaker architecture lacked obvious ornamentation, as the church's precepts—later formalized by the Millennial Laws—forbid cornices, moldings, and other embellishments that were not necessary to the function of the building. However, many of the Shakers' eighteenth-century

neighbors also avoided needless flourishes, largely because they lacked the time, energy, or money to invest in such luxuries. The result is that many Shaker buildings possess an appealing familiar quality—they represent a style we are comfortable with, yet they also signify a step toward the "less-is-more" aesthetic that characterizes so much of modern design.

In addition to wooden clapboard, the Shakers used stone and brick, especially for outbuildings. Settlements in Ohio and Kentucky, which were somewhat removed from their Brethren in the East, used brick even for meetinghouses, though that was frowned upon by the Elders of New Lebanon, with whom Elders in other settlements were required to consult before making major decisions. The shortage of timber in those western settlements made the preferences of the easterners moot, however, and the abundance of stone and clay in that region for firing brick settled the matter.

The Kentucky climate also contributed to certain architectural traditions that evolved in those communities. Hot summer months meant that a southern flair prevailed through necessity: ceilings were higher and hallways wider, to promote good air circulation. Shaker buildings in the East also adopted many of these conventions, as fresh air came to be considered important for maintaining good health.

Kentucky buildings also feature arches, a form rare in other Shaker buildings. This motif appears to be a purely regional preference, with no functional basis, though it imparts a softer look to the buildings that is more in keeping with the architecture of the surrounding area.

The Shakers typically designed their structures according to the community's needs rather than in response to the architectural fashions of the day; indeed they worked without any intent of building something beautiful to look upon. And yet, despite this apparent lack of focus on aesthetics, the buildings the Shakers made are exceptionally graceful in their proportions and stunning in their symmetry. Simplicity, order, and fine workmanship were all paramount in Shaker design, and in striving to meet these ideals, the Believers could hardly help but create remarkably beautiful buildings.

OPPOSITE: Work buildings, like New Lebanon's tannery, were less prominently placed in the landscape, set behind the front line of dwellings, offices, and meetinghouses. The size of these buildings, however, makes a bold statement about the prosperity of the industries that were housed inside.

One of the most notable things about a Shaker village was its orderly and prosperous appearance. In an era when many towns and villages grew up haphazardly, with buildings added wherever there was space, Shaker villages were thoughfully planned. The meetinghouse, which functioned as a worship space, was at the heart of the community, with each family's complex of buildings within walking distance. Principal dwellings, shops, and offices lined the major roads that ran through Shaker villages. In tidy rows behind these streetside buildings were secondary buildings: ice houses, additional workshops, and the like. While these more prosaic buildings were certainly less prominent, they were just as thoughtfully designed and well-maintained as their more visible counterparts.

Surrounding the Shakers' simple dwellings and work-shops was a neatly laid out patchwork of herb gardens, vegetable plots, field crops, and orchards.

FIRST AND FOREMOST: THE MEETINGHOUSE

In keeping with the Shaker ideal of communalism and with efforts to discourage vanity, few builders—or carpenters or craftspeople, for that matter—signed their works. No individual was to draw attention to his or her accomplishments; rather, all work was to be an expression of devotion to God and service to the community. Despite this admonishment, one builder stands out among the Shakers: Moses Johnson was a master carpenter

RIGHT: Brother Moses Johnson designed and oversaw the building of nine meetinghouses just like this one, which is still in use at Sabbathday Lake. Meetinghouses were generally located at the physical center of Shaker villages, bringing members together for communal worship.

who oversaw the construction of ten Shaker meetinghouses. All of Johnson's meetinghouses followed the same basic form, reiterating the commitment to unity of worship.

The meetinghouse was the most important building in any Shaker village. It was typically one of the first buildings constructed in any community and, because of its hallowed nature, an inordinate amount of time and energy was devoted to its creation. Although meetinghouses were of central importance to the Shakers, and were all designed with open space to accommodate large numbers of people and to allow for movement during the spiritual dance, conspicuous symbols of religion were absent: there was no cross atop the building, no church bells, no altar. In many ways, the meetinghouse looked remarkably similar to other Shaker buildings, and in fact, when the community outgrew a meetinghouse it was sometimes used for another purpose.

New Lebanon, New York, boasted the first meetinghouse built by Moses Johnson, and it served as a model for those in other communities, just as the layout of the village and the organization of the society were adopted by other settlements. Seven meetinghouses, including New Lebanon's, are clearly documented as the work of Johnson, while three others—those at Hancock, Alfred, and Sabbathday Lake—are attributable to Johnson chiefly by virtue of Shaker oral tradition. Because the Shakers kept track of such details as the builder of a structure or the craftsman of a particular piece of furniture only as a matter of efficiency in business records, and not to celebrate the work of the individual, identifying the work of particular craftsmen can be difficult.

In January of 1786, the New Lebanon meetinghouse was complete, and Johnson moved on to aid other communities in need of a meetinghouse. Note that the meetinghouse at New Lebanon today is not Johnson's original; the extant meetinghouse was built in 1824 to replace the first building when it became too small. (The original meetinghouse remains standing but currently serves as the residence for Darrow School's headmaster.) In his wake, Johnson left a series of buildings that were elegant in their proportions and stunning in their functionality.

OPPOSITE: Set between the Ministry Shop (left) and the meetinghouse (right) is a bell that is rung each Sunday during the summer to call the Shakers' worship meeting to order at Sabbathday Lake. The bell was brought to Sabbathday Lake from Alfred when that community closed in 1931.

All of the meetinghouses Johnson built featured simple rectangular footprints, white-painted wooden clapboard, and distinctive gambrel roofs. This type of roof was usually reserved for meetinghouses; simple gables were ordinarily used for other buildings in the community. The gambrel roof is a hallmark feature used by the Dutch who colonized the Hudson River Valley, where the original Shakers had also settled, but architectural historians point out that it was a form used by the English as well, and that Johnson's roofs more closely emulate the deep-eaved British rendition.

Johnson's meetinghouses featured a pleasing symmetry that was conveyed, in part, by the separate entrances for men and women. A balanced window arrangement and flanking chimneys situated at either end of the building also contributed to the overall sense of order. The chimneys were fed by small woodburning stoves, which the Shakers found both warmer and more fuel-efficient than fireplaces.

Considered sacred space, meetinghouses were painted white, a symbol of purity. According to the original Millennial Laws, the meetinghouse was the only building that was to be painted white, but as time passed some Shakers moved away from strict adherence to this policy. Several shops at Sabbathday Lake, for instance, were also painted white.

A picket fence, painted white to match the meetinghouse, stood between it and the road and held it slightly separate from the rest of the village. Two gates, one for the Brethren and one for the Sisters, were situated directly in front of the appropriate entrance, providing a pleasing sense of balance to the scene.

Today, only four of Moses Johnson's original meetinghouses are still in existence—those at Sabbathday Lake, Maine; Canterbury, New Hampshire; New Lebanon, New York (currently used as a residence); and Hancock, Massachusetts. The building that now stands at Hancock Shaker Village, however, is not original to that site. This lovingly restored meetinghouse was built for the community at Shirley, Massachusetts, but was moved in 1962 and now stands in the location originally designated for Hancock's own meetinghouse.

TOP: The meetinghouse at Pleasant Hill lacks the distinctive gambrel roof that characterized many of the eastern meetinghouses. Because Brother Johnson did not make his way to the western communities, the meetinghouse architecture found there differs markedly.

BOTTOM LEFT: Like fences throughout the communities, the meetinghouse fence at Sabbathday Lake draws a tangible border between the Shakers and the World. Shakers built miles of picket, board, and stone fences, which served a practical purpose as well: fences kept animals penned in where they belonged and out of places where they might prove a nuisance.

BOTTOM RIGHT: Shaker landscapes were laid out in careful, rectilinear patterns. Here, Canterbury's Ministry Shop (foreground) is lined up directly behind the meetinghouse. The proximity of the shop to the meetinghouse made it more efficient for those in the Ministry to accomplish their many duties.

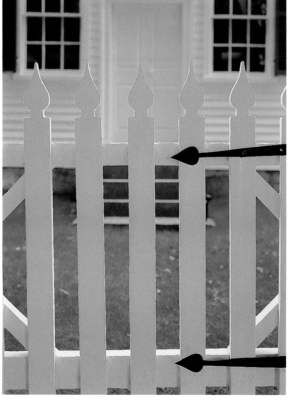

RIGHT: Set in the doorway of the Canterbury Meetinghouse, this rocker is part of a romantic vignette. But the realities of the chair's design are less than charming: while the chair might be comfortable, its short rocker blades mean that if one rocks forward or back with any energy the chair will tip over, leading some to call it the "suicide rocker."

ABOVE: Canterbury Shaker Village's stately meetinghouse was one of ten designed and built by Brother Moses Johnson. It provided ample space for worship, housing for visiting Ministry, and a physical and spiritual focal point for the community.

While Moses Johnson is perhaps the best-known name associated with the building of Shaker meetinghouses, his were not the only to be constructed. Johnson never traveled to the western communities, and the architecture there differs noticeably. Two of the meetinghouses in the West—one in South Union, Kentucky, and another at Whitewater, Ohio—were made of brick, despite the disapproval of the Ministry at New Lebanon. They also lacked the gambrel roof of Johnson's meetinghouses.

As Shaker communities grew, a few of the original meetinghouses designed by Johnson became too small, and they were often replaced by buildings constructed on a different model. One of the most dramatic, the second meetinghouse at New Lebanon, has an arched roof and vaulted ceiling and holds as many as 1500 people.

THE BELIEVERS AT HOME: SHAKER DWELLINGS

ABOVE RIGHT: Shaker dwellings are a commanding presence in a rural landscape. The Center Family Dwelling at Pleasant Hill was constructed of native stone and designed in the building tradition of the upland South.

OPPOSITE: Horizontal courses of limestone in Hancock's 1830 Brick Dwelling minimize the building's six stories and help anchor it in the landscape. This extraordinary building boasts 100 doors, 245 cupboards, 369 drawers, and 3,194 panes of glass, inside and out.

While the Shakers are not the only sect to promote celibacy, they alone practice this principle while living together with members of the opposite sex. Shaker dwellings generally had several floors—and some were as many as five or six stories—but Believers generally did not segregate the sexes on different floors. Instead, men and women lived on opposite sides of a corridor. There were some exceptions, however: during the early twentieth century, Brethren at Hancock lived on the main floor of the 1830 Brick Dwelling while Sisters occupied the upper floors.

The Shakers referred to their living quarters as dwellings, and these buildings were designed, like meetinghouses and other buildings, for efficient communal life. The early Shaker dwellings in the East showed the influence of Federal and Georgian architecture, but with an even greater purity of line and simplicity of construction. Most superfluous architectural embellishments were eliminated, leaving a simple rectangle with a remarkable symmetry brought about by the dual entry doors and separate staircases. Some dwellings featured an additional wing at the rear, if the family was of sufficient size to require it. Other dwellings lacked the distinctive dual entries, and instead featured a single entrance with separate stairs

leading to it; still others had a sole streetside entrance with doors at the sides or rear of the building intended for separate use by Brothers or Sisters. Like other elements of Shaker architecture, the number and kind of entrances related in part to local building traditions.

As Shaker membership swelled in the early part of the nineteenth century, Believers were compelled to add onto existing dwellings or to build progressively larger residences, some of which housed as many as a hundred people. These multi-story edifices perhaps resemble college residence halls more than any other type of institutional or domestic architecture.

Building materials and paint colors of Shaker dwellings varied according to the region, but the Millennial Laws advised that wooden buildings that fronted the street were to be light in color, while those relegated to the back could be red, gray, or brown. As the nineteenth century drew to a close, however, the Shakers abandoned many of these admonitions.

OPPOSITE: Shaker villages are colorful, both inside and out. The brick of Hancock's dwelling (in the background) was originally painted red and the shutters green; the Sisters' Shop (in the foreground) was yellow.

ABOVE: Many buildings in Shaker villages were used as dwellings. Here, at the Girls' Shop at Sabbathday Lake, young girls lived, played, and worked under the supervision of adult Shaker Sisters.

One of the most refined Shaker dwellings is located at Enfield, New Hampshire. This magnificent structure is one hundred feet (30.5m) long and boasts four full stories and two half stories. Built of granite blocks, the dwelling at Enfield represents a feat of architecture that drew the admiration of visitors from all over New England.

The date stone on the only extant dwelling at South Union, Kentucky, was laid in 1824. The building was actually under construction from 1822 to 1833. Built entirely of red brick, it did not, like most dwellings, feature separate streetside entrances for the Brethren and Sisters. Instead, this dwelling had a single front door that had two sets of stairs, leading up from either direction.

ABOVE: The Center Family Dwelling at Pleasant Hill exhibits the same Federal influences seen in other regional architecture of the period. With more than forty rooms, the massive size of the building reflects both the exceptional size of Shaker families and their prosperity.

Pleasant Hill, Kentucky, also features an important Shaker dwelling. Referred to as the Center Family Dwelling or the Great Limestone Dwelling, the building was under construction for a full decade. With more than forty rooms on four stories, the dwelling also features a small cupola that sits slightly off-center on the roofline. The cupola opens onto a small, balustraded widow's walk, another unusual feature for a Shaker building, but not uncommon in that region.

Both these Kentucky dwellings had multipaned windows topped with stone lintels and flanked by dark exterior shutters that closed to protect the glass when rough weather threatened. Shutters also acted as screens during summer months when windows were open.

A Shaker House?

Unlike most domestic architectural styles, which have been fairly broadly applied to homes across the country and were originally designed for family use, authentic Shaker architecture is not particularly accessible to modern homeowners. For one thing, the Shakers built in relatively few communities, and for another, the buildings today are largely either preserved as museums or have already been converted to another use, typically a commercial or institutional use. Finally, and perhaps most importantly, the dwellings were intended for the efficient communal life of a large number of people rather than for the comfort of a small family.

There are, however, a great number of homes that are in keeping with the less-is-more design philosophy of the Shakers, and these make lovely settings for Shaker-style furnishings—whether authentic antiques or careful reproductions. Simple clapboard or shingle-style houses with clean lines and gabled roofs make fine choices. Classic homes in the Georgian or Federal style—which prevailed at the time the Shakers were building their first meetinghouses, dwellings, and shops—are especially appropriate. Indeed, any house modeled upon the principles of simplicity, cleanness of line, and editing of superfluous ornament may serve as a fitting backdrop for a refined collection of Shaker pieces.

ABOVE: This Maine home, located not far from Sabbathday Lake, features the sense of balance and symmetry found in many Shaker dwellings, but has been constructed on a more modest scale.

BARNS AND SHOPS: THE ARCHITECTURE OF LABOR

Barns were a common sight in the Shaker landscape, as Believers worked the land to provide for their communities. Each village was self-sufficient—in terms of basic survival at least—and the Shakers raised their own crops and kept livestock. Unsurprisingly, the same sense of order and pure functionalism that pervaded dwellings and meetinghouses imbued Shaker barns with an air of purpose and efficiency.

Whenever practical, Shakers built their barns into hillsides, which allowed them to enter the barn from two or three different levels. In this way, hay could be driven into an upper level and pitched down into a central mow, and from there distributed to the animals.

Perhaps the most memorable of all the Shaker barns is the Round Stone Barn at Hancock, Massachusetts. A circular two-story stone structure is capped by a twelve-sided wooden story; above it stands a hexagonal cupola. This efficient design allowed a haywagon to enter through the upper barn door, unload hay into the center, circle the barn, and head out the same door, never having to back up.

RIGHT: Two workers dressed in traditional garb lead horses back to their stalls at Pleasant Hill, now a living history museum. Shakers embraced technology enthusiastically, and stopped using horses for plowing their fields once the more efficient tractors were available.

OPPOSITE: The 1826 Round Stone Barn at Hancock Shaker Village is the only round Shaker barn. Built to house dairy cows, the design allowed for efficient storage of hay as well as systematic feeding and milking of the cows.

Shaker barns had to support enough livestock to sustain the entire family, and thus these barns were many times larger than their neighbors'. The barn at New Lebanon, for instance, was nearly 300 feet (91.5m) long and five stories tall. It stored grain and hay in addition to housing cows on the main level.

In addition to farming, Shaker Brethren and Sisters worked at a number of industries, including carpentry, cabinetmaking, smithing, basket weaving, spinning, and so on, and each of these occupations required its own dedicated space. And the Shakers showed no less attention to detail in the construction of their shops than they did in the building of their meetinghouses and dwellings.

Into their workspaces the Shakers incorporated any new technology they thought could make life better and work more productive. Unlike the Amish, with whom they are often confused, the Shakers welcomed time- and labor-saving devices. Once tractors were invented, for instance, the Shakers abandoned their old-fashioned ox- or horse-drawn plows, and built special sheds to house these new conveniences.

The Trustees' Office represented another kind of work building found in a Shaker village. Though the Shakers desired to withdraw from the World, they realized that cutting all ties was impractical. To limit and control the amount of contact that Believers had with the World, they designated the Trustees' Office as the place where visitors could enter to do business. Here, guests could also get a meal or a night's lodging if they had traveled some distance to do business with the Shakers.

Toward the end of the nineteenth century, the Shakers made a concerted effort to update some of their buildings to reflect their awareness of changing times, focusing especially on the buildings most likely to be visited by outsiders. In order to project an image of prosperity to

ABOVE: In many Shaker villages, walls were built using the rocks and stones cleared from fields. The tanyard at Pleasant Hill is enclosed by a fine stone wall built by the Brethren, who engineered miles of such walls.

ABOVE: Many buildings constructed in Kentucky's Shaker villages were made of stone or brick because those resources were more plentiful than timber. The Trustees' Office at Pleasant Hill, shown here, is a fine example of a brick building erected by Shaker Brethren.

the World, the Shakers abandoned many of the restrictions placed upon them by the Millennial Laws and added spindles, brackets, moldings, mansard-roofed cupolas, and all manner of adornment to their offices, bringing the buildings firmly into the Victorian era. In fact, these buildings have a distinctly un-Shakerlike appearance. Nevertheless, it is the straightforward demeanor of the earlier buildings that defines the Shaker aesthetic and remains most appealing to us today.

Opposite: The one-room schoolhouse used by the Shakers at Sabbathday Lake now holds the community's library of materials written by and about Shakers, including original diaries and account books, letters, historic photographs, imprints, and ephemera.

Top: Formerly an ox barn, Sabbathday Lake's expansive barn today houses sheep, cows, and pigs. The structure opens on two ground levels: tractors and other farm equipment are kept in the bay in the foreground, while sheep and cows occupy the lower level. Pigs are penned in the section to the right.

Bottom Left: The Shakers appreciated fine tools, and elevated toolmaking to an art. These late-nineteenth- and early-twentieth-century farm implements hang beneath a row of straw hats, equally necessary equipage for a farm worker.

Bottom Right: A view of the pasture is framed by the Spin House and Boys' Shop at Sabbathday Lake.

THE LANDSCAPE

Shaker villages were characterized by an overwhelming simplicity, and it is this orderly quality that we find so irresistible today. Part of the enduring charm is undoubtedly the luxuriant gardens cultivated by the Shakers. As with so many of their other lifeways, the Shakers followed the Millennial Laws regarding their garden planning; the Laws advised Believers to "lay out and fence all kinds of lots, fields, and gardens, in square, where it is practicable."

The Shakers did not garden for pleasure or for the beauty the plants brought to the landscape, however. For the Believers, a garden was valuable only for what it could yield in practical terms: food, seasonings, and medicines. While they grew what we today would consider ornamental flowers, each had a purpose. Roses were grown and their essence distilled to make rosewater, a flavoring for baked goods. To discourage Sisters from making an "idol" of the bloom, they were admonished to cut roses entirely without stems, so that they would not be tempted to accent their dresses with the blossoms. Poppies were also cultivated in vast fields, as opium was important medicinally and was a highly profitable commodity for the Shakers.

Toward the end of the nineteenth century, the Shakers eased some of their traditional restrictions, and began to grow purely ornamental flowers, which they sometimes brought into the dwellings to beautify the rooms. Botany was a passion of the Victorians, and though the Shakers never embraced the lavish ornamental gardens that were in fashion in the latter half of the nineteenth century, they did teach the girls who attended their schools—Believers and nonbelievers alike—to tend flower beds, as this was considered an important part of the education of females.

Herbs were among the most important plants grown in Shaker gardens, and were cultivated both for culinary and for medicinal use. Like other cooks of the eighteenth and nineteenth centuries, the Shakers experimented with the subtleties of herbs to lend variety and zest to their dishes. Among the herbs found in Shaker kitchen gardens were anise, basil, caraway, chervil, coriander, marjoram, oregano, parsley, rosemary, summer savory, and thyme.

OPPOSITE: Medicinal gardens were often grown near Shaker dwellings. The purple coneflower in the foreground is the healing herb echinacea.

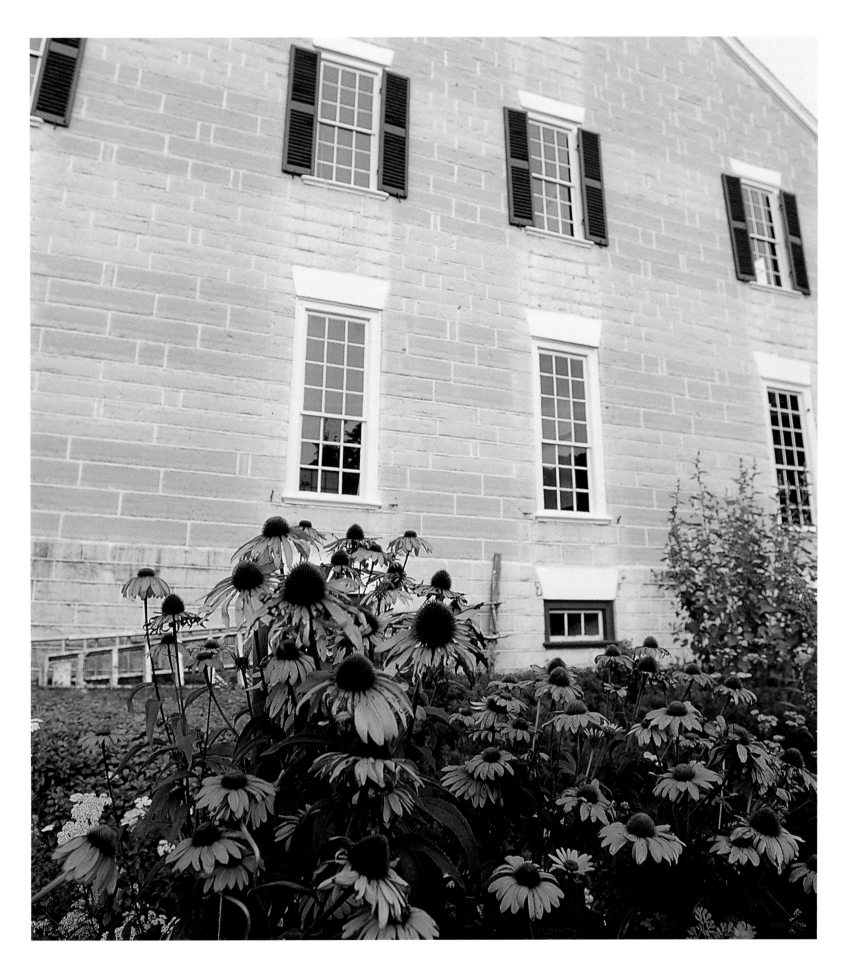

OPPOSITE: The Shakers tended their gardens with great care, and were rewarded with excellent harvests. Neat and organized, this demonstration garden at Pleasant Hill overflows with the bounty typical of Shaker vegetable plots.

ABOVE: Harvesting, drying, and processing herbs was serious business for the Shakers, who depended upon them for both seasonings and medicines. In some villages, the sale of herbs and/or herbal remedies was an important part of the community's livelihood.

Healing herbs were even more critical to the Shakers, as Believers relied largely on herbal medicine for their health care. Doctors were scarce among the Shakers, but each community had an infirmary, and there the Shakers went to be treated for various ills. Some of the Shaker herbal remedies came to be quite famous for their efficacy, and eventually the Believers began packaging and selling these remedies to the World. In some villages, herbal medicines became a significant source of income, and the Shakers there grew vast quantities of herbs to satisfy commercial demand. In addition to preparing and selling herbal remedies directly to the public, Shakers also supplied pharmaceutical companies with bulk herbs to be processed into medicines.

Nineteenth-century medicine was filled with charlatans and quacks all trying to make a quick dollar, often at the expense of public health, as their remedies were often dangerous in addition to being ineffective. The Shakers, however, were well respected for their honesty in business and for the purity of their medicines. At a time in history when "medicines" often consisted of nothing more than alcohol, the Shakers took great care to ensure that the remedies they sold were carefully labeled and undiluted by additional substances. Sisters took great pains when harvesting medicinal herbs, gathering only one type at a time so as not to mix them.

Herbs were an important cash crop for the Shakers and served an important role in their ability to care for their communities, but were only a small part of the cultivation they undertook each year. With families numbering as many as a hundred people at the height of Shakerism, the Believers had a great many people to feed each day. Vegetable gardens provided for the family table, and were cultivated near the dwellings in order to make transport of food to the table most efficient.

Among the vegetable crops grown in Shaker family kitchen gardens were beans, beets, cabbages, carrots, celery—which was cultivated for its seeds and leaves as well as for its stalks—cucumbers, onions, parsnips, peas, spinach, squash, and tomatoes. When the Shakers grew more than they needed to feed their families, there was a willing market waiting to buy up their excess.

In addition to the kitchen gardens that the Shakers maintained for their own use, they grew vast crops for seed, which they sold to the World in market-savvy packaging. These commercial tracts were planted and maintained separately from the gardens intended to provide for the Shakers, and were treated as an agricultural industry. As with household chores and the tasks associated with their other various industries, the Shakers were always looking for new and improved ways of growing crops. They were among the first to experiment with hybridizing vegetables, attempting to grow larger and healthier specimens, reduce disease, and increase yields.

The Shakers were also devoted to their orchards. They grew fruit trees of many types, including cherry, plum, peach, quince, damson, pear, and apple. They prepared many dishes

OPPOSITE: The demonstration herb gardens at Hancock Shaker Village provide a glimpse of some of the medicinal and culinary plants traditionally grown in Shaker gardens. Bordering the garden on one side is the brick Poultry House, its solid construction testament to the importance of the poultry business at Hancock.

RIGHT: This contemporary demonstration garden at Hancock Shaker Village shows many of the varieties of vegetables that were grown in Hancock's historic gardens.

TOP: A wooden seed crate details on its label the heat-tolerant varieties contained inside, including bunch beans, collards, okra, and spinach, among others.

BOTTOM LEFT: Packets of seeds are beautifully organized in this hinged wooden case. Note the printing on the dividers and the edges of the case, specifying the proper place for each group of seeds.

BOTTOM RIGHT: This collection of seed crates shows off the eye-catching display labels designed at New Lebanon and Enfield. The Shakers would ship their seeds in such crates to merchants at the beginning of the season. Later in the year, the Shakers would visit the merchants, who worked on commission, to collect remaining seeds and make any payment due.

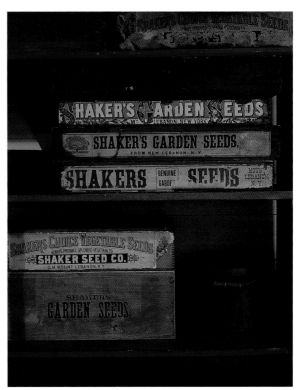

using fresh fruit in season, but when the harvest began in earnest, they had more than they could possibly use in the short term. The Shaker sisters preserved jar after jar of fruit, jams, and sauces, intended for use during the long winter and through the summer until the next harvest. They also dried fruits, which they added to savory dishes and desserts.

While the Believers grew many different types of fruit trees, the queen of the Shaker orchard was the apple tree. They cultivated different varieties for different purposes, using some for eating, some for baking, some for cider, and some for applesauce. Among the varieties most widely grown were Pippen, Jonathan, Ben Davis, Baldwin, Rhode Island, and Winter Banana.

Along with seeds and herbs, orchard fruits provided a reliable source of income for many Shaker communities. As the nineteenth century advanced and the railroad system spread across the nation, Shaker fruits could be shipped across the country to an ever-eager public that appreciated the quality that the Shaker name guaranteed.

ABOVE: Today, the tranquil landscapes of restored Shaker villages belie the busy farms and centers of industry they once were.

Chapter Three

THE SHAKERS AT HOME
Interiors

A consistent use of rectilinear patterns is one of the hallmarks of Shaker architecture and furniture design, and is readily apparent in this series of upper-floor rooms in the meetinghouse at Sabbathday Lake.

RIGHT: Arches provide effective structural support, and are especially prevalent in stone and brick buildings. Shaker builders in Kentucky used arched windows more consistently than their New England counterparts, in keeping with southern architectural traditions. This elegant dormer window appears in the upper hallway of a dwelling at Pleasant Hill.

OPPOSITE: Interior passages featured arches as well, as evidenced by this graceful archway at Hancock Shaker Village. White plaster, fine woodwork, and the peg rail are also characterstic of Shaker interior design.

While the Shakers were averse to any embellishment added "for fancy," they were not opposed to celebrating the beauty of nature in their designs, and strove to incorporate God-given ornament wherever they could. They celebrated sunlight and fresh breezes, and invited these blessings of nature into their dwellings, shops, and meetinghouses with high ceilings, wide corridors, and multitudes of windows. Painted surfaces were not considered to be "fancy" but merely common habit inside and outside Shaker villages. Prior to the Civil War, most household woodwork, built-in cabinetry, and furniture was painted. Tastes began to change during the Victorian era, and even Shakers stripped and varnished their furniture and woodwork. Prior to that time, it was not uncommon to find highly figured woods covered with paints.

Above all, the Shakers were pragmatic in their approach to designs of all kinds, seeking to simplify their tasks and eliminate unnecessary clutter as well as save steps in their daily

routines. In their interiors, the Shakers endeavored to create rooms that were eminently functional, and in the process created spaces that we today view as exquisite in their simplicity.

DESIGN AND DETAILS

Shakers live their religion every day of their lives, and the floor plans and architectural details of their buildings—from their meetinghouses to their dwellings to their barns—reflected this integration of practicality and spirituality.

Meetinghouse interiors were intended to facilitate the spiritual dance that helped define the Shakers from the first. In the beginning, the dance had been characterized by a frenzied whirling and what was described by many witnesses as "gyrations," but in the decades after Mother Ann's death, the steps were formalized by Father Joseph Meacham. He instituted a series of coordinated steps forward and back, which allowed the Shakers to express their unanimity of belief and purpose in harmonious movements.

To keep the floor open for spiritual dance and song, the ground-level interiors of meetinghouses were built with no pillars or other vertical supports. All ceiling and roof support was maintained by enormous trusses that were visible only in the attics.

Benches reserved for guests were set at the front of the room or sometimes were built into the walls along the sides, and were the only furnishings that were not movable. Throughout most of Shaker history, the public was welcome at their services, and at some points there were more people of the World in attendance than there were Shakers. Many visitors came from sheer curiosity, but others truly wished to learn more about Shaker beliefs.

Additional seating was afforded by rows of benches, where the Brothers and Sisters typically sat, or, in some cases, by chairs. Shaker chairs were specifically designed to be light and portable, and could be picked up and hung on pegs to clear the way for ritual dance; meetinghouse benches were likewise easily moved, so they could be efficiently cleared out of the way. Meetinghouse benches were often backless, and could be stacked if necessary.

The design of the meetinghouse typically provided space on the upper floors for the Ministry's living quarters, and sometimes offered office or work space as well. The Ministry lived apart from the rest of the community so that they could maintain objectivity with regard to their charges and so that they could focus on the group's spiritual well-being.

Dwellings, too, were marked by an interior design well tailored to the sect's religious beliefs. While men and women were believed equal, the practicalities of maintaining a celibate life meant that they should be segregated most of the time. The Shakers provided opportunities for contact between men and women through regulated social meetings, called Union Meetings, but limited these relationships and took care to remove undue temptation. Many of the Shaker dwellings were scaled to provide accomodation for up to a hundred people, and so were comprised of multiple stories. But instead of separating the Brothers and Sisters by floor

RIGHT: Even today, the meeting-house at Sabbathday Lake is used for the Shakers' public worship during the summer months. The spacious room is set with rows of benches, with sections that face each other to accommodate both Brethren and Sisters. The built-in benches in the foreground were used by onlookers in the nineteenth century. Today, the public sits in the rows behind the Shaker Family, spilling over to the built-in benches only when the service is full.

the Shakers assigned men to one side of the hallway and women to the other. Believers saw this proximity as testament to the strength of their faith. They realized, however, that human virtue had its limits: for this reason, halls are usually quite wide, which prevented Brothers and Sisters from coming into close physical contact in the corridors. As with exterior entrances and staircases, Brothers and Sisters used segregated interior staircases, which led from the bottom of the building to the upper retiring floors.

Many of the staircases themselves are works of art. Delicate free-standing spirals or beautifully symmetrical pairs of staircases with sinuous polished banisters grace the interiors of dwellings and meetinghouses throughout all the Shaker villages. Like other architectural elements, staircases are free of superfluous ornament yet crafted with great care, allowing the inherent beauty of the contours to prevail.

Refraining from the use of elaborate architectural details saved the Shakers considerable expense and, ultimately, lent their interior spaces a refreshing simplicity that is as pleasing today as it was when originally built. Much of the appeal of Shaker spaces is achieved through basic features like windows and woodwork, reduced to their most elemental forms.

Because Shaker buildings were so massive, Believers needed to find creative ways to admit light and air into their interiors, and to heat them as well. The Shakers preferred stoves to fireplaces, which were the norm in the houses of most of their New England neighbors, because

OPPOSITE: Brother Micajah Burnett designed this rather un-Shakerlike staircase—actually one of a pair—for the Trustees' Office at Pleasant Hill. The spiral form, together with handrails that are carved, not bent, distinguish this from more traditional Shaker staircases. Skylights on the top floor allow natural light to stream into the building.

RIGHT: Borrowing from the spare and practical attics at Hancock Shaker Village, this contemporary space makes use of a minimalist, freestanding staircase, and is flooded with light from attic skylights.

the stoves were more fuel-efficient and gave off heat more evenly. In many of the spaces, the stoves rested on stone slabs to provide a measure of fire safety. Many early dwellings were constructed with fireplaces for heating and cooking, but as soon as it was practical the more efficient woodstoves were installed.

Transoms above doorways allowed light from rooms to filter into hallways and interior rooms, and offered increased ventilation as well. Interior windows were another innovative way to invite sunlight into spaces that were removed from exterior walls. Stairwells and closets benefited from these practical architectural touches, as well as more visible and well-used spaces.

The Shakers also made use of skylights, adding these now-popular features long before they became widely fashionable. Large windows set into roofs filled attics with natural light, and some dwellings even featured "double" skylights: paned windows set into both the roof and the floor of an upper attic, which allowed sunlight to filter through to a second attic below. Skylights and interior windows were more than a cosmetic architectural flourish, though—they reduced the risk of fire by decreasing the need for candles or lanterns in these rooms. Fire posed such a threat, in fact, that in the Millennial Laws of 1845, Shakers were forbidden from carrying open flames; they could carry a candle or lamp only if it was secured inside a lantern.

Fresh air was another integral aim in Shaker interior design. Shaker wisdom held that a good flow of clean air was essential to health, and the builders incorporated features intended to promote air circulation in their rooms. In addition to the transoms that allowed air into the rooms and halls at ceiling level, Shaker rooms often featured baseboards that were drilled with holes to encourage air flow near the floor.

The Shakers employed not only specialized windows such as transoms and skylights, but also a multitude of exterior windows. For example, the dining room of one dwelling at Hancock boasts eight oversized windows (each with twelve over twelve panes) that welcome sunlight in from three directions. These windows feature special engineering that allows them to be easily removed for cleaning. Wooden thumbscrews and a narrow strip of wood fasten the

OPPOSITE: Details of Shaker architecture appear sculptural in form. In the dining room of Pleasant Hill's Center Family Dwelling, the multilighted arched transom and the hexagonal base of the central post are aesthetically pleasing as well as functional.

sashes to the window frame; unscrewing the hardware and removing the wooden piece releases the window. The window frames themselves flare gracefully, inviting maximum light and air into the room.

Throughout the buildings in Shaker villages, a number of distinctive architectural details impart visual interest to the rooms while maintaining an emphasis on simple practicalities. Wainscoting and chair rails were designed to protect the lower portion of plaster walls from the inevitable nicks and scuffs that would occur when benches, chairs, or other furnishings were moved, and to provide pleasing contrast to stark white plaster walls.

The interior architectural detail perhaps most associated with the Shakers is the peg rail, a strip of wood outfitted with turned pegs that runs around the interior of a room about six feet (1.8m) above the floor. Peg rails became standard architectural elements in every type of Shaker building, from meetinghouses and dwellings to workshops and offices, and pegs were used to hang items as varied as hats and clothing, chairs, tools, mirrors, baskets, and even clocks. In rooms that might otherwise be described as austere, the peg rail serves as appealing visual relief.

While peg rails were ubiquitous throughout Shaker communities, other interior architectural features varied from region to region. In Kentucky's stone and brick buildings, for example, interior doorways through load-bearing walls were often arched rather than squared, as is typical in other Shaker settlements. This classical feature lends a particular grace to the Kentucky dwellings.

RIGHT: Hallways in southern Shaker dwellings, like this spacious example at Pleasant Hill, were generally wider and featured higher ceilings than corridors in northeastern dwellings. The hotter, more humid climate of the South required architectural features that promoted good air circulation.

All Shaker dwellings, however, featured abundant built-in storage, most of which was located in the kitchens, retiring rooms, and in spacious attics. Cabinets, drawers, and cupboards in various sizes, shapes, and configurations were used to store everything that the family needed, from off-season clothing and linens to dishes.

Floor-to-ceiling cupboards in a dining room might house plates, serving pieces, and eating utensils, while those set into walls in corridors were likely to hold bedding, linens, clothing, and an array of household items. Cupboards and drawers were often numbered, and logs detailed what each compartment held. With so many people living together in one space, it was essential that everyone be able to find each necessary item. Mother Ann herself had often admonished her followers to "Provide places for all your things, so that you may know where to find them at any time, day or night." Time spent searching for mislaid utensils, tools, or household items was time wasted, and time wasted was time taken away from worship.

Drawers were often built in graduated sizes, lending visual interest as well as solving a practical problem: the larger lower drawers housed heavier objects. If the built-in storage extended higher than the person using it might be expected to reach, a small step-stool would be set nearby. Built-ins also satisfied the Shakers' interest in cleanliness, because they had no horizontal surfaces on which dust could collect. As Mother Ann was fond of saying, "There is no dirt in heaven."

ABOVE RIGHT: Storage areas in the upper floors of Shaker dwellings provided ample—and orderly—space for surplus and off-season clothing and linens. Drawers were often marked with individual names or numbers to facilitate efficient return of items to the owner or room from which they came.

THE SHAKER PALETTE

The Shakers developed traditions with regard to the use of color that were later codified by the Millennial Laws. White paint was more expensive than red, brown, tan, or yellow, and so was usually reserved for the exterior of the most important building, the meetinghouse. Blue, likewise, was costlier and more difficult to obtain, and so it dressed the trim of meetinghouse interiors. The Millennial Laws ordained that the woodwork inside the meetinghouse be painted "bluish," which was typically interpreted by the Shakers as a deep aquamarine.

Walls in meetinghouses, dwellings, and shops were almost universally white plaster, though in some meetinghouses they were painted a pale shade of blue. The woodwork in buildings was most often painted: yellows and reds in dwellings; blues, greens, or yellows in workshops. The doors of cupboards and drawer fronts in built-ins were often painted to contrast with the case—the use of red and yellow together was common.

Above: The blue painted woodwork and white plaster in this modern bath were inspired by the Shaker palette. Other borrowed elements include efficient built-in cabinetry, a peg rail, and small accents such as oval boxes, a straw hat, and a mirror hung from one of the pegs.

Floors might be a rich yellowish hue, though sometimes they were stained a deeper reddish tone. The Shakers' wood floors were admired by their contemporaries for their high shine, which was achieved only by polishing—the floors were never varnished, as varnish was to be applied only to handrails and movable furnishings.

While the Shakers would have used interior colors only in certain proscribed ways, home decorators today can apply this rich traditional palette more flexibly. For a traditional Shaker look, paint walls a clear white, and leave wooden doors, windows, chair rails, and other trim its natural color. Or experiment with the deep blue-green, warm reds and oranges, chocolate brown, and mustard yellow of Shaker interiors by painting entire walls or trim with these earthy colors. Whatever color scheme you choose, complement it with clean-lined furniture and minimal accents for an aesthetic that is both refined and easy to live with.

OPPOSITE: This "flying" staircase stands between two attic floors in Hancock's 1830 Brick Dwelling, and harbors built-in drawers off both sides. Even in the attics, which were not frequented by the public, Shaker craftsmen took great care to create efficient and beautifully designed passages between floors.

TOP: Built-in drawers in this attic space in the Center Family Dwelling at Pleasant Hill are lit by an innovative skylight. This allowed access to the storage without the use of candles, which posed a risk of fire.

BOTTOM LEFT: The Shakers' tradition of built-in storage translates very well to modern spaces. A contemporary walk-in closet incorporates many of the same features seen in Shaker rooms, including an extensive use of wood, a mix of cupboards and drawers to hold items of different sizes and shapes, and a good source of light, here accomplished with recessed spot lighting.

BOTTOM RIGHT: A sleek bedroom corner evokes the Shaker love of simplicity and efficient storage but also borrows from a Japanese sensibility, evidenced by the window treatment and wall sconce as well as the dresser-top display of favorite objects.

COMMON SPACES

The interiors of meetinghouses and dwellings share a sense of light and air, coupled with a dedication to clean lines and clutter-free living, that foreshadow modern interior design movements. But there were layout demands associated with Shaker buildings that relate to few other examples of domestic architecture. Homes in the World typically included rooms for receiving guests and places for family members to relax, but Believers had little use for parlors, and few Shaker dwellings incorporated them. Union Meetings—small gatherings where men and women talked, prayed, and sometimes sang together in the evenings—generally took place in retiring rooms, the dormitorylike rooms in which Shakers slept.

Customary common spaces in a Shaker dwelling included a dining room and a meeting room. Dining rooms needed to be large enough to serve all members of the family at once, and, like most other spaces, were arranged so that men and women did not mingle. All daily meals were segregated, with Brethren dining on one side of the communal dining room and Sisters on the other. Double doors into the dining room provided for separate entry by the Brethren and Sisters, with each door leading to the appropriate side of the room.

Shakers were expected to eat quickly and in silence, having first knelt and said prayers of thanks. The Sisters who cooked the meal also served the food and waited at table. In some Shaker dwellings, the dining room and the kitchens were on the same floor, making for reasonably efficient serving, but in others the dining room was located above the kitchens. When the kitchens were in the basement, dumbwaiters transported the food to the dining room, and the dining level usually featured a small pantry or supplemental kitchen to make serving easier.

Each dwelling also included a spacious room for evening family worship. These family meetings were held during the week and lasted from shortly after supper until the family retired for the night. In addition to evening worship, the meeting rooms were used for Sunday services when inclement weather prevented the family from traveling to the community's meetinghouse.

OPPOSITE: A glimpse through the doorway between the dining room and central hall in Hancock's 1830 Brick Dwelling clearly shows several classic architectural features of Shaker buildings: the dual entry simplified the separation of Brothers and Sisters, who remained segregated even in communal spaces; a transom over the doors allows natural light from the dining room to pass into the hall, and twin peg rails in the hallway allow everything from coats and hats to chairs and brooms to be hung there.

Perhaps the most "public" of all the Shaker buildings were the Trustees' Offices, which were specifically designed to entertain visitors from the World. And just as Believers updated the exteriors of their offices with more frequency and with greater attention to the architectural fashions of the day, they took equal care with the offices' interior design. In some instances, the interiors of Trustees' Offices bore little resemblance to other, older Shaker buildings, as the offices were renovated with the latest Victorian styles in mind, including elaborate hardware and heavily carved wood moldings and medallions.

THE KITCHENS

Shaker women cooked for large numbers of people, most of whom worked at agriculture or industries that were physically demanding, and thus hearty meals that could be efficiently produced were a priority. Sisters rotated shifts in the kitchen, with each serving about a month at a time.

Kitchens were typically small complexes consisting of a group of related rooms, including a large main kitchen, a separate room specifically for baking, a serving kitchen, a buttery, storage rooms, a scullery, and a Good Room—a special pantry where the best foodstuffs were stored. Also near the kitchens were areas for water storage and a cooling system that helped preserve food stored in the pantry.

The Shakers embraced simplicity in their cooking just as they did in their architecture and furnishings, yet they also advocated the use of technology as long as any advances represented real improvements and were not merely novelties. For example, Shakers were among the first to install running water and electricity in their buildings. Everything in the Shaker kitchen was designed to produce food in quantity, and the Shakers busied themselves acquiring the very best commercial cooking equipment. They invested in large commercial ranges, and later in such innovations as griddles and deep fryers. These were fueled by wood in a firebox located beneath the griddle or fryer surface.

OPPOSITE: The cooler rooms in the basements of Shaker dwellings were often set aside for the storage of fresh and preserved foods, and sometimes served as work spaces for the Sisters' impressive canning projects. Here at Hancock Shaker Village, empty jars stand ready to be filled with fruit, while rows of preserved fruits and vegetables fill the shelves behind the work table.

TOP: Shaker kitchens were large, busy places that sometimes served hundreds of meals in a day. Long surfaces were required to efficiently prepare the mostly seasonal food that made up the bulk of the Shaker diet.

BOTTOM: Contemporary yet warm and appealing, this kitchen incorporates use of a number of Shaker influences: efficient built-in cabinets and drawers, clean lines and surfaces, and ample natural light. Gleaming brushed stainless steel appliances are conveniences the Shakers would have appreciated for their easy-to-clean surfaces and their time-saving qualities.

OPPOSITE: This kitchen/dining area draws upon a tradition of Shaker ingenuity with its wealth of built-in cabinetry and tall, multi-paned windows. Heat generated by the woodstove is well distributed by a two-story open area surrounding the exposed stove-pipe.

In some Shaker dwellings, particularly in the South, massive fireplaces were used for cooking as well as for heating the kitchen (though, even in the South, Shakers adopted cookstoves and woodstoves by the 1830s), and were fitted with enormous iron kettles for soups, stews, puddings, or vegetables. Ovens large enough to bake dozens of loaves of bread at a time featured relatively sophisticated systems of dampers designed to control the temperature of the oven. Many kitchens had separate ovens for bread and pies, with pie ovens often designed in round shapes to echo their contents.

In these vast kitchens, the Shakers also launched large-scale canning and preserving operations, putting up fruits and vegetables, sauces and jams to sustain them through the long winters or to supply to the World for profit.

RETIRING ROOMS

Bedrooms, called retiring rooms by the Shakers, were spartan by today's standards, but were in fact quite comfortable given the norm in eighteenth- and early-nineteenth-century America. The sleeping arrangements in Shaker dwellings were similar to those in dormitories, with men occupying one side of the hallway and women the other. Four or five people typically shared a room, though the numbers might range anywhere between two and eight.

Retiring rooms offered space for the Brethren and Sisters to sleep and to store their clothing and a few toiletries, but the

OPPOSITE: Shaker retiring rooms were neat and orderly. Each room contained several beds, a washstand, chairs, and the ubiquitous peg rail, used to hang a variety of items, such as mirrors, clothing, and extra chairs.

RIGHT: A country attic bedroom recalls the simplicity of Shaker domestic décor, but carries out the principles on a more achievable scale.

ABOVE: The more cluttered look popular during the Victorian era is evident in this retiring room in the Ministry Shop at Sabbathday Lake. Patterned textiles and floor coverings complement the painted trim and the more decorative furniture of the period. Note, too, the elaborate iron supports under the clock shelf on the right wall.

Shakers spent little time awake in these rooms and the interior design reflected that. All Brethren and Sisters were required to go to bed at the same time unless they had leave from the Elder or Eldress. In the morning they dressed quickly and left their retiring rooms soon after being awakened. Union Meetings took place in retiring rooms, and on these occasions Shaker men and women would bring chairs into the room and line them up facing each other in two segregated rows. The rows were spaced a decorous distance apart, and the men and women conversed quietly and then sang or prayed until bedtime. This was typically the most activity a retiring room saw.

Apart from the setup required for Union Meetings, furnishings in retiring rooms were minimal. Each room featured a narrow bed for each occupant (in the early days even double beds—for two occupants), a rocker, a chair, a washstand and mirror, a candlestand, and built-in furniture. If elderly Shakers resided in the room, additional rocking chairs were provided for their use.

Room-sized woven carpets were commonly laid in winter, taken up and cleaned in spring, then stored until fall, and scatter rugs were also used, but other creature comforts were few.

Though closets were usually absent in eighteenth-century houses, Shaker retiring rooms often featured them. Perhaps it is not surprising, given the Shaker devotion to good storage. There is also some speculation among historians that larger closets were used as dressing rooms to protect the modesty of Shaker Brethren and Sisters.

Late in the nineteenth century, when a Victorian sensibility swept the country, the Shakers were likewise affected, though to a lesser degree than the people of the World. In this era of excess, even Shaker retiring rooms were more likely to include lavish furnishings and carpets. These later rooms, in general, possess less of the characteristic flavor of the classic Shaker interiors so admired today.

In all their efforts, the Shakers showed themselves to be efficient and open to technological advances, and the design of their interiors proved no exception. They were often the first residents in a region to modernize with conveniences like electricity, running water, and indoor plumbing, and their dwellings and shops were filled with labor-saving devices and innovative designs that made tasks more efficient and allowed the Shakers to devote more of their time to worship.

With their appreciation of natural features such as sunlight and fine wood grain, their sensitivity to elements such as symmetry, balance, and proportion, and their fine use of color and graceful lines, the Shakers created interiors that speak to our modern love of clean and airy yet highly functional spaces.

ABOVE RIGHT: Shakers made maximum use of stovepipes to conduct heat throughout building interiors. Stoves are more efficient heating units than fireplaces, and the length of exposed stovepipe further enhances the heating power.

Chapter Four

FURNITURE
A Celebration of Simplicity

Like all Shaker endeavors, furniture making was inextricably linked with tenets of the faith. The Brethren put Shaker philosophies to work in their designs, believing that "all things must be made…according to their order and use." Superfluous decoration was studiously avoided and the beauty of functionalism allowed to shine through. Utilitarianism was the chief principle upon which Shaker designs were based, and that which was useful was considered inherently beautiful.

The Shakers reduced the design of each piece of furniture to its essential form, and in so doing they invoked the inner beauty of each object. For the Shakers, the essential thing was also the most useful thing, and the furniture they created embodies the "form follows function" rule at its purest.

Because the Shaker way of life required that furniture be moved from room to room for different purposes, and dictated that it sometimes be cleared away entirely, many pieces of furniture were designed for portability. Chairs were sometimes hung from peg rails, and thus had to be quite light, so as not to pull the pegs from the rail. Because of its spare design and light weight, the furniture has a delicate look that seems at odds with the Shakers' need for sturdy pieces that could withstand regular use by a multitude of family members. But fine Shaker craftsmanship lent all the furnishings a fundamental strength that served the community well.

Shaker Brethren often worked in an assembly-line fashion, with many different individuals all contributing to the good of the whole. This communal method of work was adopted in part for efficiency's sake, but it also ensured that every Brother could develop skills necessary

PAGE 100: This unique double desk is emblematic of Shaker design in that it is simple and practical yet beautifully crafted. Intended for use by a pair of Trustees at New Lebanon, the desk provides space for storing writing utensils, papers, and other necessary supplies.

ABOVE RIGHT: Shaker craftsmen used a myriad of hand tools to create the many beautiful products they made for themselves and for sale to the World. The individual attention paid to each object contributed to its quality and durability.

ABOVE: This setting in the 1830 Brick Dwelling at Hancock Shaker Village shows the continuity between furniture and architecture. Note the consistent use of frame and panel construction in the deep window frames and the doors of the built-in cupboards. The same method of construction is found on many similar freestanding pieces created at Hancock.

to ensure the continuity of labor and success of the industries. It made good sense that no one person held the burden of an individual labor.

This communal approach to design and construction also resulted in a finished piece that was uniform, a trait that appealed to the Shakers. In their work, the Shakers aimed for perfection, for they viewed all of their labor as a part of their worship. In their communities, they attempted to create an earthly mirror of heaven, and thus strove for perfection in everything they did. Furniture makers in Shaker communities consistently worked with the best tools and steadily refined their techniques until they could be counted among the finest craftsmen ever to produce wood furnishings.

While the Shakers believed that no man or woman should possess things better than their Brethren or Sisters, and so strove for uniformity, they did tailor their furnishings to accommodate people of various sizes. With their typical practical approach, they realized that one size did not fit all and that people were more likely to perform efficiently when given furnishings that fit their forms and suited their needs, thus foreshadowing the movement toward ergonomic design in modern office and household furniture.

Because the design of both buildings and furniture followed the same Shaker principles—chiefly the quest for perfection and the elimination of the inessential—the resulting buildings and furniture complemented one another beautifully. The Shakers created interiors and furnishings that worked together stylistically, anticipating the whole-environment designs of later architects like Frank Lloyd Wright and Charles Rennie Mackintosh. Perhaps this approach, which we view as a contemporary one, is part of the reason that Shaker furniture and household goods are so valued by collectors today: the pieces presage modern movements, where economy of line and a clean aesthetic, as well as an awareness of overall surroundings, are celebrated. However, Shaker pieces, with their association with country styles, are often warmer than modern furniture and interiors, which typically make use of industrial materials and may appear somewhat cold.

CHAIRS

Chairs were the most common type of furniture made by the Shakers, as they were needed for meetinghouses, dining rooms, and retiring rooms, as well as in workshops, offices, and kitchens. But the Shakers also produced these pieces for sale to the people of the World. By 1789, the Shakers at New Lebanon were selling their chairs to outsiders, and the industry eventually became a valuable source of revenue. While they may have sold a select number of other types of furnishings at various points in their history, chair making was the only Shaker furniture industry of note.

OPPOSITE: A classic tape-seat rocker sits beside a refined tripod once used as a candlestand. The economy of line and absence of lavish detailing that marks Shaker architecture is apparent in the furniture designs as well.

From single-slat, low-back dining chairs to classic four-slat rockers to diminutive seats for children, Shaker chairs came in a variety of sizes and styles to suit all the members of the community. But all the chairs benefited from the Shakers' commitment to superior craftsmanship and their insistence on making furniture that was lightweight, sturdy, of simple design, and sized and shaped to fit the human body.

The most common Shaker chair was the three-slat ladder-back side chair, so today this is the piece most available on the antiques market and is quite often reproduced as well. The slats on the chair back are gently curved to cradle the human form, while each slat was typically a bit wider than the one above it, creating a supportive yet comfortable back. Many Shaker chairs were built with a slight backward tilt, to better fit the contours of the human body.

Chair legs and the posts used for the back were turned carefully on lathes, with the top of the posts capped by either rounded or pointed finials. Each post was made from a single piece of wood, which resulted in chairs that possessed a fundamental strength, though they were delicate in appearance. The legs were delicately tapered and without feet, eliminating any unnecessary wood and producing finished chairs that were lighter and also less expensive because they used less wood.

The gentle tapering of the legs lent Shaker chairs a sophistication unmatched by other chairs made at that time. Because of these innate qualities of design, Shaker chairs required no added adornments such as carving or decorative painting, which the Shakers avoided in any case because of their faith. Despite their lack of obvious ornament, the chairs are among the most beautiful ever produced. Believers had no objection to painting their furniture in solid colors, however, as it helped finish and preserve the wood, and chairs were often painted in yellow, salmon, or red.

Around the 1850s, the Shakers began to construct chairs with what they designated as "tilter feet." These ball-and-socket feet were installed on the bottom of the back posts and allowed the sitter to lean back in the chair, lifting the front chair legs from the floor but keeping the back

OPPOSITE: This early country side chair, with its woven wood-splint seat, simple ladder-back form, and pronounced finials, is a forerunner of the chairs manufactured by Shaker craftsmen.

OPPOSITE: A lovely set of reproduction Shaker chairs features the cushion rail that was added to many Shaker chairs late in the nineteenth century. This bar, which stretches between the two back posts of the chair, allowed a cushion to be secured to the chair back.

TOP: In this contemporary approach to design, a Shaker-style trestle table and ladder-back chairs are combined with upholstered window seating to provide an inviting dining area.

BOTTOM LEFT: The Shakers created chairs tailored to the needs of all members of their community. These chairs are scaled for children, and indeed the Shakers outfitted entire rooms with miniature furniture intended for efficient use by young people.

BOTTOM RIGHT: Many Shaker chair posts terminate in a decorative finial, or pommel, and some communities developed distinctive finials. This "egg in a cup" style of finial is typical of those found on chairs produced at South Union.

feet completely flat. This marvel of design was apparently intended to permit the Shakers to indulge in their habit of leaning back in their chairs without creating gouges or scuff marks on the polished pine floors. A similar device is found today on students' desk chairs and on some office chairs.

By the middle of the nineteenth century, the classic period of Shaker chair making was passing. With a wider market demanding ever more product, the Shakers began to streamline some of their processes and to rely on machinery that helped them mass produce chairs. While the designs continued to embody the simplicity for which the Shaker had become so well known, some of the exquisite care that had previously been taken with each piece was now lost. The chairs became relatively standardized and were widely available in stores and through mail-order catalogs.

At about this time, the Shakers also began labeling their chairs with a distinctive trademark designed to protect the Shaker name. Counterfeit Shaker furniture intended to capitalize on the Believers' designs and reputation for quality had begun appearing in the marketplace, and despite the slight decline in quality in the mid-nineteenth century, Shaker pieces still exceeded most others in sturdiness and craftsmanship.

Beautifully woven tape seats were one Shaker innovation, but it is not their single achievement in the evolution of the chair. Revolving chairs, known to Believers as "revolvers," are one of the important Shaker inventions that remains with us today in the form of our ubiquitous swiveling office chairs as well as piano stools, bar stools, and the like. The Shakers never patented this invention (they felt that patents were contrary to their ideals of communal ownership, and rarely filed for them), and few of us sitting in our comfy swivel chairs today know that we can thank the Shakers for this convenience.

The Shakers made both swivel stools and revolving chairs in various sizes and styles, depending on where and by whom the chair would be used. These "revolvers" were much in demand by women for use as sewing chairs, while the backless versions made ideal piano stools.

TAPE SEATS

Shaker chairs are well known for their handsome woven-tape seats, a style distinctive to the Believers. The first tape seats were made in the second decade of the nineteenth century. Before that time, chair seats were woven with hickory splints or with cane, a typical feature for American country chairs.

Tape seats appealed to the Shakers for several reasons: they were comfortable, durable, attractive, and easily woven. The colored tapes, often woven in contrasting bright and neutral shades, also lent the no-nonsense, clean-lined chairs a lively air.

Shaker Sisters wove the chair seats, at first using tapes they made with hand-spun and dyed Shaker yarns. Later, the Sisters purchased tapes made of wool and cotton twill—these twill tapes were less costly, and the Sisters could eliminate from the process the time they would have spent making the tapes themselves. The purchased tapes continued to be woven by the Sisters in traditional checkerboard or herringbone patterns.

ABOVE: It was common to see a variety of chair styles in a Shaker community. Some villages did not produce enough chairs for their own use and so purchased them from other communities. Woven tapes, often in contrasting colors, were used to create comfortable seats, and sometimes chair backs as well.

While the Shakers were not inventors of the rocking chair, they certainly embraced the form with a vigor not previously seen in America. The Shakers took excellent care of all members of their communities, being particularly concerned with the elderly and those in frail health, and rocking chairs were one of the comforts provided to them. Over time, because other Brethren and Sisters also found them to be comfortable, rockers became part of the typical furnishings of Shaker retiring rooms.

Shaker rocking chairs typically featured four back slats and were made both with and without arms. By the middle of the nineteenth century, the Shakers began making what was known as the "cushion-rail" rocking chair. This chair was similar to its precursors except that it also featured a rod situated above the top slat. A cushion was secured to the rod, and hung down the back of the chair to provide additional comfort. Not surprisingly, many of the more traditional Shakers disapproved of rocking chairs for the able-bodied in general, and of the cushion-rail rocker in particular, as it provided no special benefit to the community and was devised solely for the comfort of the individual. As comfort became a more important require-ment, rocking chairs with either a taped or upholstered back were also offered.

BENCHES

Benches are perhaps the quintessential Shaker furnishing. They seated the multitudes in the meetinghouses and originally graced the table sides in early Shaker dwellings. When Shakers first came to live together in spiritual communities, there were rarely enough chairs to seat the entire group at meals or for worship, and benches were a simple and economical solution: they provided seating in abundance (and more people could always be crowded onto a bench, unlike a chair) and they were relatively easy and inexpensive to make. Many backless benches could also be stacked to create extra floor space when necessary.

Once their initial seating needs were met, the Shakers began crafting chairs for their dwellings, but they continued to use benches in the meetinghouses until the end of the

OPPOSITE: Shaker-style rocking chairs are graceful additions to bedrooms of any décor, and provide beautiful accents as well as restful places to sit.

nineteenth century. Typically, meetinghouse benches were about ten feet (3m) long and were used to seat both Shakers and visitors to the service.

Basic and austere, backless New Lebanon benches were among the simplest of Shaker designs: they featured robust planks stretched atop two or three legs with arched bases. Utilitarian to the utmost degree, New Lebanon benches were not particularly comfortable, and today these antique and reproduction benches are generally reserved for areas of the home, such as an entryway, where people will not be required to sit for long periods of time. They are also pressed into use as coffee tables or to hold stacks of books or other items.

A graceful backed bench produced primarily at Canterbury and Enfield, New Hampshire, was far more aesthetically pleasing as well as more comfortable for those seated on it, and this bench is widely reproduced today. Dating to the mid-nineteenth century, the bench was outfitted with a slightly canted back that seemed to visually lift it from the ground. Each seat was created from a single piece of wood, but was subtly shaped for the human form.

ABOVE RIGHT: Typical of the benches produced at Canterbury and Enfield, this exquisite meetinghouse bench possesses an ethereal look that belies its superior strength.

TABLES

Unlike Shaker chairs, which were made both for use by community members and for sale to the World, tables were usually produced for the Shakers' use alone. Shaker tables varied widely in size, depending on their intended use, and ranged from small round-topped tripods to massive dining tables.

Trestle tables were popular and effective because they could seat the maximum number of people, since there were no traditional legs or gatelegs in the way. These tables were most often featured in the vast communal dining rooms of Shaker dwellings.

Like most of the furniture and other items the Shakers made, the Believers improved upon the version they first copied. Colonial American trestle tables featured a center rail, which ran the length of the table, halfway between the tabletop and the floor. Shaker Brethren began constructing their tables so that the brace ran just beneath the tabletop, allowing plenty of space below for leg room.

In addition, Shaker trestle tables possessed the same fineness of proportion and delicacy of feature that pervaded the Shakers' other furniture designs, whereas early American trestle tables tended to be heavy, with an obvious, solid construction. The design and choice of wood used for Shaker trestle tables varied somewhat from village to village, with each community making use of locally available hardwoods.

Shaker dining tables, like all their communal pieces, were oversized, typically at least ten feet (3m) long and three feet (1m) wide, though some were as long as twenty feet (6m).

ABOVE RIGHT: The extraordinarily long, tapered legs of this modern occasional table have been inspired by the design and fine craftsmanship of small Shaker tables.

The tables made for the Ministry, who dined separately from the rest of the community, were smaller, intended for use by just four people.

In addition to dining tables, Shaker Brethren produced a variety of four-legged tables and smaller tripods, which were used for particular chores or to facilitate jobs in specific industries. Many were designed for use by more than one person at a time. There were drop-leaf tables with drawers for sewing; enormous, heavy-topped tables for cutting bread; and side tables with added galleries for a variety of handwork.

Legs on these tables were either squared, tapering down to plain feet, or turned in a simple fashion, and the overall design of the tables was exceedingly graceful. Today, these exquisite four-legged tables, most of which are more appropriately proportioned for modern homes than the large trestle dining tables, are sought after by collectors for use as nightstands, end tables, occasional tables, or consoles.

Three-legged tables were also an important part of the Shakers' repertoire, and some of these are among the most elegant examples of Shaker craftsmanship. The tripods that the Brethren crafted for use in retiring rooms—to hold candles or other necessities—feature round tops and exquisitely turned legs. These lovely pedestals are most often made of cherry. Some communities produced well-proportioned square- or rectangular-topped candlestands.

More utilitarian tripods were also produced, and these were used for tasks such as sewing or seed-sorting, though they might also be used as reading stands. These functional pedestals were of simpler construction and featured modest chamfered legs.

Desks

Shaker writing desks are relatively rare. They were not standard furniture in Shaker dwellings, as writing was discouraged as an act of individualism. In their wholly communal lives, the Shakers were not supposed to record their own thoughts for posterity. Such writing as was necessary, chiefly record-keeping and communications between villages, was mostly the province of

Opposite: This writing desk was cleverly crafted to look like a chest of drawers: the second drawer pulls out and drops down to create a writing surface, and conceals a series of cubbies and small drawers. Such "deceptions" are rare in Shaker furniture, as Believers generally advocated honesty in all aspects of their lives, including the construction and decoration of furniture.

Above Right: A personal office space can incorporate many of the basics of Shaker design with clean-lined, efficient furnishings and adequate storage. Here, a desk that has been influenced by the design of Shaker pieces and a reproduction chair create a small but eminently functional work space.

the Deacons and Deaconesses and the Elders or Eldresses. Though writing was generally forbidden for "common members," discretionary use was allowed by the 1821 Millennial Laws, which specified that "writing desks may be used as far as it is thought proper by the lead."

Practicality dictated that the Elders keep community records, however, and desks in a variety of styles were made for them, including laptop desks, which could be easily transported when the Ministry needed to travel to another Shaker village. Beneath the slanted tops of these portable desks rested an array of compartments that housed all the writing accoutrements the Elders would need—pens, paper, and bottles of ink.

Other desks were slant-topped, with simple tapered legs. Because existing Shaker desks vary in size, with little duplication, some historians speculate that most were custom-made for specific Elders.

The Shakers also crafted desks that featured a cupboard on top and a drop-front surface for writing. Still another sort of desk was used for sewing. With flat tops for holding the Sisters' handiwork, these pieces had niches and drawers to hold scissors, thread, needles, and other sewing notions. Many of these desks were outfitted with drawers on the side, an ingenious feature that allowed the sewer access to the stored items without having to push back from the desk and search beneath the desktop.

Because desks were often located in the Trustees' Office, which was exposed to visitors with greater frequency, later examples were more elaborate than the simple desks of the eighteenth and early to mid-nineteenth centuries. The desks produced in the western settlements also tended to be more lavishly designed, with spindles commonly adorning the outer desk edges.

Aside from the community Elders, the only segment of the Shaker population that commonly used desks was schoolchildren. The desks made for students were a pared-down version of the adult slant-topped desks, but unlike adult writing desks, those for children were made to seat six to eight. In addition to the children of converts and those orphans the Shakers took in, children of nonbelievers were welcome at many of the Shaker schools, and local parents made use of this education resource.

While the Shakers believed firmly in education for all children, boys and girls, they were equally determined about the type of book learning that was appropriate. Not surprisingly, they favored a basic education that prepared children with the skills they were likely to need in life: reading, writing, spelling, arithmetic, and geography. According to one Shaker Brother, life, which is short in any case, "ought not be spent in acquiring any kind of knowledge which can not be put to good use." The strictly utilitarian desks that the Shakers created for children reflected that no-nonsense philosophy. And just as the Brethren and Sisters worked separately, so, too, did male and female children attend school separately.

OPPOSITE: Inspired by the Shakers' furniture as well as by their work ethic, this office desk has an ample surface that can be extended significantly by the use of drop leaves, a favorite Shaker feature. When work piles up or space for decorative items is inadequate, the front and side leaves can be put into service.

ADDITIONAL FURNITURE

Shaker lifeways also required several other types of furnishings, and perhaps most important among these was the washstand. The Shakers were dedicated to the Biblical ideal that cleanliness is next to Godliness, and washstands were typically provided in each retiring room. In addition, some dwellings featured communal washrooms, which housed a number of these functional pieces. Most included a cupboard below for storing the essentials of hygiene; the top was bordered on three sides by a lip, which prevented the pitcher and bowl from being pushed off the side or the back and kept water from splashing onto the walls.

Mirrors were also provided in most retiring rooms, but their size was regulated by the Millennial Laws, which noted that they ought not exceed twelve by eighteen inches (30.5–45.5cm). While the Shakers were to maintain a neat appearance, vanity was soundly discouraged.

Chests of drawers were not common in Shaker dwellings, especially early in the communities' history. Instead, they relied on vast built-in cupboards and drawers for their storage needs. By the early 1800s, however, the Shakers had begun to make chests of drawers, and their designs are widely copied today for use in bedroom suits that include dressers and bureaus. Many of these, rather than being reproductions, are simply inspired by the plain but elegant designs of Shaker chests of drawers.

Blanket chests, however, were quite popular for storing bed linens and extra blankets. Early "six-board" blanket chests were most often made of pine painted a deep red or yellow. Over time, drawers were added to these lift-top chests, first one, then two, and finally three. Locks were not common on these chests, or in fact on any type of Shaker cupboard or drawer, as all community members were presumed to be trustworthy.

Finally, Shaker beds did not differ much from those in use in the World at the time. The earliest were often double beds, hence the usefulness of the admonition to "sleep straight." By the mid-nineteenth century, Shaker craftsmen were producing more uniform single beds.

OPPOSITE: Communal families needed large case pieces to meet their storage needs. This massive chest of drawers was made at New Lebanon and is now on display in the Center Family Dwelling at Pleasant Hill. A stepstool nearby kept the uppermost drawers accessible.

ABOVE: This modest but comfortable bed belonged in a retiring room for Shaker Sisters. Room settings were relatively spare, and a retiring room needed only a few furnishings. This one includes only a bed, a reading stand, and a table and chair for light writing duties or hand work.

OPPOSITE: Early Shaker beds featured simple wooden frames with rope supports for the mattress. This modern four-poster bed—with its spare, Shaker-inspired lines—harks back to those times.

They were typically set on wheels, to make cleaning beneath them easier, and were outfitted with mattresses atop stretched ropes. The queen- and king-sized beds today that are commonly designated as Shaker-style borrow from Shaker design traditions, but have little basis in history. Yet they make lovely accompaniments to the host of other furnishings modeled after Shaker designs, and suit the lifestyles of modern couples in a way that authentic reproductions could not hope to do.

Whether the pieces are valuable antiques, faithful reproductions, or simply inspired by the Shaker commitment to fine craftsmanship and economy of line, Shaker-style furnishings are beautiful additions to every home. Installed in traditional rooms or in sleek contemporary settings, Shaker-style pieces create a warm and welcoming atmosphere for today's families.

RIGHT: Drawers in graduated sizes maximize the versatility of this cupboard over drawers. Side tables with generous overhangs had multiple uses, including as writing surfaces or sewing desks. This table is unusual for the casters on its legs—not many Shaker tables featured wheels.

Chapter Five

THE DETAILS OF LIFE
Household Goods

Shaker "accessories" were not frivolous home accents, but instead were pieces crafted specifically to enhance the utility of the dwelling or shop. Like Shaker-made buildings and furniture, household items were designed first to be useful, and to the Shakers their beauty rested chiefly in their ability to serve.

Many of the woven baskets, brooms, oval wooden boxes, kitchen serving pieces and utensils, sewing notions, and other household items that the Shakers made to help them in their daily chores were sold to people of the World as well, though the Shakers typically satisfied their own needs for goods first. While these items were initially sold in shops at the Trustees' Office, where worldly people visited, there was such demand for these objects outside Shaker communities that owners of local general stores began to carry them as well. During the last quarter of the nineteenth century and through the first quarter of the twentieth, Shaker Sisters often traveled to East Coast resorts to sell their wares.

The household items the Shakers produced share with their furniture an elegant, streamlined look that presaged modern design principles. Along with many twentieth-century designers, Shaker craftsmen were dedicated to the ideas that form should follow function, that local materials were best, and that a simple design was more efficient and therefore more beautiful than one that was overly complicated or excessively adorned.

As with everything they did, the Shakers invested in their crafts a sense of spirit that appears to live in the objects. Honesty of construction, attention to the least detail, and a sincere belief that labor was a form of worship shine forth from virtually everything they made. Today, Shaker household goods are widely collected, and many are faithfully reproduced or have been used as a point of inspiration for a variety of beautiful home accessories.

PAGE 128: Oval boxes and carriers were produced in many sizes, allowing them to fill almost any need for storage of small items. This collection from the Fruitlands Museum shows the range of sizes and some of the paint finishes. Many carriers were lined with fabric, outfitted with emerges, beeswax, and needle cases, and called "sewing baskets."

ABOVE RIGHT: Bonnet forms allowed Shaker Sisters to work efficiently in three dimensions. Today, any such small sculptural items make charming home accents.

OPPOSITE: While tinware was in evidence throughout the dwelling, most of these pieces were bought by the Shakers rather than produced in their own shops. Tinware was especially common in the dairy and the kitchen: these shallow pans were used to cool fresh milk quickly.

BOXES AND CARRIERS

After ladder-back chairs, wooden oval boxes are perhaps the best known and most admired of all Shaker products. These delicately fashioned boxes were being made by the end of the 1700s and, within a century, were manufactured in the Shaker communities at New Lebanon, New York; Alfred and Sabbathday Lake, Maine; Canterbury and Enfield, New Hampshire; and Union Village, Ohio. Some boxes were also made at Harvard and Shirley, Massachusetts.

First known as "nests" of boxes because they were created—like today's mixing bowls—in graduated sizes, oval boxes held everything from sewing notions to nails to foodstuffs. Early sets were made up of twelve boxes, though later sets featured fewer, typically five, seven, or nine.

Maple was favored for the bentwood sides of boxes, but other woods, such as birch, were also used. The wood was soaked in hot water until it became pliable and could be easily molded around a form designed for the purpose. Box lids and bottoms were typically crafted from pine, a soft wood that was in abundant supply.

"Swallowtail" joints lend the boxes a graceful appearance, but also serve a practical purpose: they allow the joints to swell and contract with changes in humidity. Tiny copper tacks, chosen because they wouldn't rust, held the end of each joint in place, and were carefully aligned up the box sides.

When finished, boxes were either varnished or painted, often in green, blue, yellow, or red. After the Civil War, most oval boxes were simply varnished. Because many were sold outside the Shaker communities, boxes with highly decorative treatments do exist, though there is little doubt that these were embellished by their new owners rather than by Believers. The Shaker Community at Sabbathday Lake continues to produce and sell oval boxes.

Oval carriers are closely related to boxes, but were typically made without a lid and with a sturdy bentwood handle. In the spirit of recycling still-useful objects, oval boxes that lost their lids were sometimes fashioned into carriers.

OPPOSITE: Shakers crafted many types of useful containers for use in their own communities as well as for sale. The oval box, with its graceful "swallowtail" joinery, has become an icon of Shaker design.

OPPOSITE: The abundance of blues seen in woodenware and early textiles leads us to surmise that it was a favored color, as it remains with today's home decorators. Blue furniture was standard in New England during the nineteenth century, when a variety of blue paints was available. Here, a country cupboard has been filled with Shaker-style boxes and other accents that share the same vibrant palette.

TOP: Thousands of wooden seed boxes were distributed to general stores in the nineteenth century. Note the bentwood handle added to the top box, transforming it into a handy carrier.

BOTTOM LEFT: The entire contents of this built-in cupboard—as well as the cupboard itself and the chair that stands in front of it—were made of wood. This multitude of wooden items reflects the fact that wood was the most common resource available in New England during the nineteenth century.

BOTTOM RIGHT: For the Shakers, oval boxes are equivalent to the plastic kitchen storage containers we use today. Like our snap-top plastic bowls, oval boxes came in multiple sizes and were sold in nests.

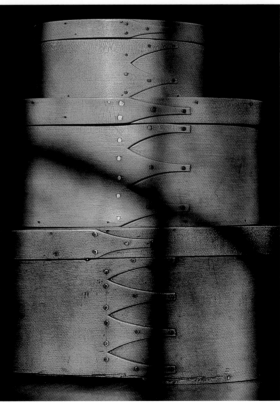

Round boxes, too, were made, but in much smaller numbers than the classic oval boxes. Because of their relative rarity, round boxes can command astoundingly high prices at auction, though oval boxes, too, are much sought after.

OTHER WOODENWARE

Other household goods, including bowls, dry measures, scoops, mortars and pestles, buckets, pails, tubs, kegs, and shovels, were also crafted from wood. Hardwoods, most popularly ash, were favored for dry measures, which sometimes featured handles and lids, though they were also made without them. Wooden scoops were made of ash or maple and, like nesting boxes, were often sold in graduated sizes, with three to a set.

Coopers' ware—namely pails, firkins, barrels, and tubs—were produced to carry or store various goods. There were containers to hold apples, butter, lard, seeds, and a host of other necessities. Butter churns can also be counted among the quality coopers' ware produced by the Shakers. Tubs were typically meant for chores like dying wool as well as for doing the washing.

ABOVE: Beautiful bowls, delicate spoons, and paddles were crafted from wood and put to constant use in Shaker kitchens, dairies, and herb houses.

TOP: Fine reproductions often exhibit the same charm and utility apparent in original Shaker pieces. This pail and piggin were produced in the crafts shops at Pleasant Hill.

BOTTOM LEFT: Barrels and baskets in an array of sizes and shapes were used to transport and store fresh fruits and vegetables.

BOTTOM RIGHT: The fine wood and smooth surface of this spade are testament to the care Shaker Brethren took in crafting their tools.

While a number of Shaker villages crafted these items, some villages opted to purchase them from other Shaker communities or from the World. As technology developed and coopers' ware was mass produced in the World, the Shakers made fewer and fewer pails and the like.

Cheese hoops were another popular woodenware item. These bentwood hoops were lined with cheesecloth and filled with curds. The hoop was then placed in a press, which gradually squeezed the liquid out until the cheese was firm. Large amounts of cheese and butter were commonly sold from Shaker villages.

OPPOSITE: Baskets were woven and used widely by Shakers, and were historically produced by many other groups as well, including Native Americans and early colonists. While many of the forms shown here would have seen daily use in the gardens, henhouse, or shops, today they are used chiefly as decorative accents.

ABOVE RIGHT: These beautiful baskets were found at South Union, and may well have been produced by Brothers and Sisters there. However, it is difficult to establish the origin of baskets because techniques and patterns were similar to those used in the World, and Shakers sometimes purchased baskets made outside the Shaker community.

BASKETS

Made in a wide variety of patterns, shapes, and sizes, Shaker baskets were used for everything from carrying laundry to harvesting fruits and vegetables to gathering eggs. Specialty baskets were also made for such tasks as catching fish or storing kindling. As with all Shaker-made things, baskets were designed specifically for certain tasks, and thus baskets used for laundry were large and shallow while those designated for egg collecting were small and deep, with a tight weave.

Most Shaker basketry was woven from splints of black ash, though white ash and some oak were also used. Work baskets made up the majority of basketry produced until the mid-nineteenth century, when more delicate, narrow-splint baskets were woven.

Shaker basket weaving, like so many of their industries, was a communal activity. Instead of a single person producing a basket from start to finish—from gathering materials to applying

TOP: Today's home decorators can pay homage to the Shaker fondness for baskets by incorporating them in a number of sizes, shapes, and styles. A shelving unit set inside the back door comfortably holds more than a dozen baskets, effectively organizing the family's gloves, scarves, outdoor playthings, and other details of life.

BOTTOM: Tens of thousands of brooms were made and sold by Shakers, ensuring America's domestic cleanliness. Reproduction Shaker brooms continue to be made today by dedicated craftsmen.

the handle—as was the practice outside Shaker communities, the Shakers divided basket-making tasks. The Brethren would harvest, split, and soak the wood, and fashion it into splints. They also carved the wooden forms used to shape the baskets, including forms for the handles and rims. These basket forms ensured that all the pieces were well-shaped and uniform, and would fit together perfectly. The Shaker women then typically wove the baskets, though some men made baskets as well.

Later, baskets known as fancy baskets were produced. The word "fancy," inherently at odds with Shaker philosophy, was used to refer to smaller baskets intended for light household use rather than those that were particularly ornate. Fancy baskets were much in demand for sale to the World, and included sewing baskets, picnic baskets, and tabletop baskets for displaying fruit.

Today, collectors value Shaker baskets for their elaborate patterns, delicate look, and natural strength, but collecting Shaker baskets can be a challenge. While it is likely that baskets were made in nearly every Shaker community, they were not marked and it can be very difficult to determine whether a basket is truly of Shaker origin. Even when a basket has a long history of use in a Shaker village, its source is not necessarily secure, as the Shakers bought baskets for community use when it was more economical to do so.

BROOMS

The Shakers' emphasis on cleanliness is well-documented, so it is not surprising that one of their chief industries was broom-making. In fact, it is a Shaker brother, Theodore Bates of Watervliet, New York, who is credited with the invention of the flat broom. Early brooms were simply sheaves of broom corn tied to a pole. When the broom corn was flattened and sewn in place, the resulting broom cleaned a wider swath of floor and was more effective at dusting corners and beneath pieces of furniture. This innovation resulted in tens of thousands of brooms being sold from Shaker villages.

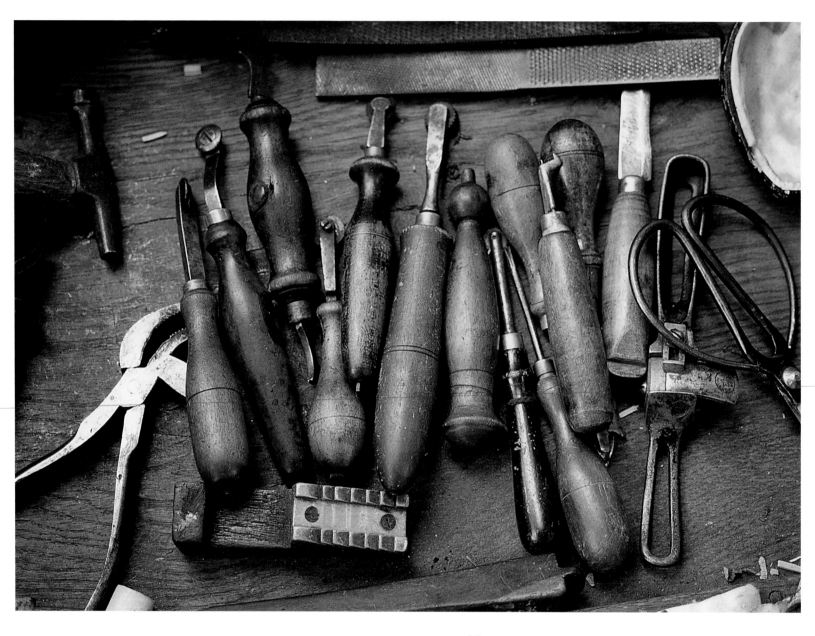

METALWORK

Metalwork was a core industry for the Shakers, for it was in their metal shops that they produced the tools and nails with which their buildings were constructed and the implements with which the farm chores were done. In the blacksmith's shop, the Brethren forged iron into nails, axes, saws, scythes, shovels, plow-irons, and horseshoes. They also "tinkered" a bit when necessary—chiefly performing repair work on the tinware items used by the community, including cake pans, sconces, pitchers, and match safes.

ABOVE: In their metal shops, the Brethren produced or repaired a variety of tools that were necessary for the workings of life in the Shaker community.

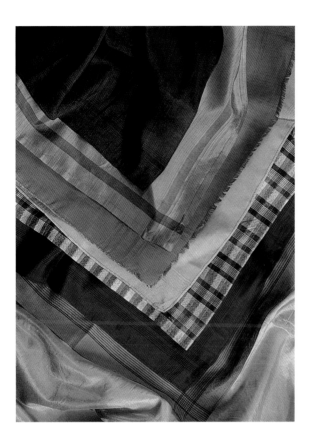
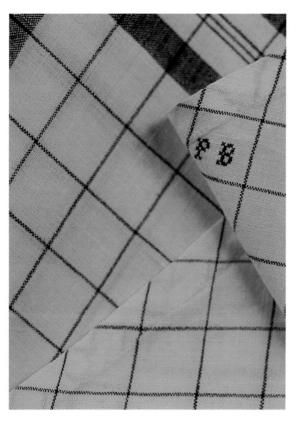

HOUSEHOLD TEXTILES

While the Shaker communities produced many textiles for their own use as well as for sale to the World, they also bought fabrics and textile goods from other Shaker villages or from outside merchants when it was more efficient or economical to do so. The textiles the Shakers did produce were similar to those of their nonbeliever neighbors, though a Shaker dwelling required towels, blankets, and bedcoverings in a far greater quantity than would a normal household. In addition, Shaker textiles were often cross-stitched with the initials of their owner or coded with a dwelling and room number that helped identify the proper place to which they should be returned from the laundry.

According to the Millennial Laws, blankets were to be of no more than two colors, though in practice a third was often added. Blankets were hemmed on the sides to provide a finished look and prevent the fabric from unraveling, but they were never fringed, like many of their Victorian-era counterparts in the World.

ABOVE LEFT: Shaker Sisters in Kentucky produced colorful silk cloth during the first half of the nineteenth century. Dresses, kerchiefs, and collars were all made from silk.

ABOVE RIGHT: Initials were commonly cross-stitched into personal clothing. Sheets, towels, blankets, and other communal property were also marked, usually with the initials of the building and the number of the room to which they should be returned from the laundry.

RIGHT: Sewing desks included a flat working surface and a variety of drawers in which to store the Sisters' needles, thread, pin-cushions, fabrics, and the like.

Quilts and coverlets, too, were sometimes used by Shakers, but were quite rare, and the few existing examples are now part of museum collections. These Shaker quilts and coverlets are more colorful than blankets, often featuring scraps of dress goods or even remnants of silk fabric produced by the Shakers. There are four quilts at Hancock Shaker Village; two are surprisingly elaborate crazy quilts made at the turn of the twentieth century.

Towels were often woven in patterns that provided texture to the cloth, rendering it more absorbent than a flat weave. While towels were frequently left white or their natural, unbleached color, border stripes and, occasionally, windowpane checks also appeared. These are found in both red and brown, but blue is by far the favored hue.

Wall hangings, similar in purpose to medieval tapestries, were also in use in the retiring rooms of Shaker dwellings. These wall coverings, which hung from the peg rails that surrounded the room, were commonly white, though some featured a blue-checked pattern. In addition to preventing chilling drafts from disturbing the occupants, the wall hangings provided visual warmth to the room.

Visual warmth, as well as actual warmth underfoot, was also offered by colorful rugs. Rags were woven or braided into strips and then were sewn together to make large area rugs or runners, reducing noise, protecting the floors, and providing warmth, but also lending welcome color and pattern to the floors of the dwelling. Rugs typically featured overall designs of diagonal stripes or bands of color, which repeated throughout the rug. At least two, and sometimes all four, edges were finished with bindings. While woven and braided rugs were most common, crocheted or hooked rugs were also made.

ABOVE RIGHT: Color was often introduced into Shaker rooms with woven, braided, knitted, hooked, or shirred rugs. This "Good" rug was made at Pleasant Hill in the mid-nineteenth century.

PICTORIAL WORKS

OPPOSITE: The swift is a device the Shakers used to efficiently wind skeins of yarn into balls. Swifts were designed to be collapsible, so that they could be folded and stored out of the way when not needed.

ABOVE: Girls in Shaker communities stitched samplers that allowed them to practice simple cross-stitching rather than the more decorative embroidery learned by girls in the World. Extant examples of Shaker samplers are few.

While the Millennial Laws of 1845 stipulated that walls of dwellings and shops be free of maps, pictures, or paintings, many such drawings were in fact made. Maps and village plans were commonly made to document the property of the Shakers, and some of these are sufficiently detailed—often including people, animals, and individual plants, as well as embellishments near the title or the borders—to be considered artwork. In the hands of some later Shaker mapmakers, what were originally simple maps intended to portray the layout of a village evolved into beautiful stylized landscapes.

However beautiful these elaborate maps may be, they cannot compare with the artistry of Shaker gift drawings. These works commit to paper the spiritual encounters that Shaker mediums, called instruments, experienced and translated visually. The gifts were believed to be sent by the spirits of Mother Ann, Jesus, or the first Shaker Elders, though sometimes were also offered by spirits of other revered figures such as Native Americans or the nation's founding fathers.

A number of early gift drawings included mysterious characters that historians designate as spirit writing; this writing was presumably translated by the person who served as the instrument of the message. Later works share many themes with other folk art of the time, including hearts and stylized flowers, trees, and birds, and employ the colors and patterns already popular in Shaker communities.

In addition to gift drawings, Shaker instruments also recorded songs and poetry that were gifted to the communities by their spiritual forbears. These songs were often shared among the communities, who might unite in song at a prescribed time of day, confident in their spiritual bond.

Gift drawings and songs began to appear in the late 1830s, at a point in Shaker history when the membership was at a remove from Mother Ann and the founding American Shakers. The reappearance of these spiritual leaders in the form of gift drawings and songs served to strengthen the faith of new converts, and resulted in a period of renewed religious fervor that lasted until the 1860s.

RIGHT: This diagram of part of the village of Canterbury displays the precision Shakers applied to most of their undertakings. In the upper left corner is the mapmaker's apology for the quality of his drawings.

OPPOSITE: The Shaker aesthetic is simple and serene, reflective of the Believers' values and way of life. Lack of unnecessary embellishment, honest construction, and supreme functionality inform all aspects Shaker design, as exhibited by the cupboard and details in this handsome tableau.

With their firm belief in the beauty of utility and their unwavering commitment to perfection in everything they made, the Shakers set a standard of design and craftsmanship that remains almost unparalleled. Their beautifully dovetailed oval boxes, graceful yet sturdy furniture, lovingly crafted implements, and simple but soaring architectural forms all reflect the value they placed on usefulness and honesty of construction. And perhaps most remarkable, given our twenty-first-century vantage point, is the fact that the Shakers lived every day the principles they held dear. They ordered their lives so that they might make the best use of the day, rising early, working efficiently and cooperatively, improving their tools and methods constantly, and stoutly resisting the foibles and frivolities of the World.

While few today would choose to live in a community that demands such discipline and exudes such overall austerity, there remains inside many of us an attraction to the simplicity, purity, and perfection to which the Shakers aspired. We yearn for simplicity in our own lives, and we readily adopt it in whatever form we find, including in our household goods. And inherent in the Shakers' smooth-topped trestle tables, colorful tape-seat ladder-back chairs, classic woven-splint baskets, yellow-stained oval boxes, and myriad other artifacts is an integrity and a serene beauty we continue to appreciate today. When we bring Shaker pieces, whether antiques or reproductions, into our homes, we not only add beautiful furnishings and accessories to our lives, we express our enduring admiration for those working in the Shaker tradition.

RIGHT: Classic white walls and golden woodwork define this passage at Sabbathday Lake, which features a handsome built-in clock. Such clocks, as well as a series of bells, helped the Shakers accomplish their tasks in an orderly progression throughout the day.

❂ RESOURCES ❂

WHERE TO SEE ORIGINAL SHAKER BUILDINGS AND ARTIFACTS

Canterbury Shaker Village
288 Shaker Road
Canterbury, NH 03224
(603) 783-9511

Founded in the 1780s, Canterbury Shaker Village sheltered roughly three hundred people at its peak in 1860; the village had one hundred buildings set on 4000 acres of land. This living history museum features craftspeople working in the traditional Shaker crafts of broom making, oval box construction, woodworking, spinning, and weaving. In addition to original buildings and furnishings, the collection includes manuscripts and photographs. The village can be toured, and the Creamery Restaurant serves full Shaker meals as well as other fare.

The Enfield Shaker Museum
2 Lower Shaker Village, NH 03748
(603) 632-4346

Enfield was settled in 1793, and remained in existence for one hundred thirty years. After the Shaker community at Enfield disbanded, the property changed hands several times, until the Enfield Shaker Museum began to acquire parcels of the property and the existing collection of Shaker artifacts. The Museum now owns the Laundry/Dairy Building, the Stone Mill Building, the West Meadow Barn, the Great Stone Dwelling, which has been outfitted as an inn, and many other original Shaker buildings, as well as fields and pastures that had belonged to the Shakers. The Museum hosts workshops, tours, exhibits, and craft demonstrations.

Hancock Shaker Village
PO Box 927
Pittsfield, MA 01202
(413) 443-0188 or (800) 817-1137

Now open as a living history museum, Hancock was originally settled in 1790. Among the restored buildings are the Round Stone Barn, the Brick Dwelling, the Trustees' Office, the meetinghouse, the Laundry, and a 1916 garage intended for automobiles. Demonstrations by artisans include weaving, basketmaking, cabinetmaking, farming, and more. The village also hosts interpretive talks, craft demonstrations, and garden tours.

Shaker Heritage Society
1848 Shaker Meeting House, Albany Shaker Road
Albany, NY 12211
(518) 456-7890

The Shaker Heritage Society was founded as a nonprofit group dedicated to preserving the Watervliet Shaker Historic District, the first Shaker settlement in the United States. It also sponsors educational programs that examine the Shakers and their influence on the region. Self-guided walking tours or guided tours by appointment explore the Church Family site, where the Society's office is located, as well as the eight remaining buildings, fields, the apple orchard, the Ann Lee Pond and nature preserve, and the Shaker cemetery. The Society also sponsors craft courses, workshops, lectures, festivals, and other events throughout the year.

The Shaker Historical Society

16740 South Park Boulevard

Shaker Heights, OH 44120

(216) 921-1201

Organized in 1947, the Shaker Historical Society is dedicated to preserving the heritage of the Shaker community and the history of Shakers in the region. The Society maintains the Shaker Historical Museum, which houses a permanent collection of Shaker artifacts and furniture. The Society offers museum tours for both individuals and groups.

Shaker Museum and Library

88 Shaker Museum Road

Old Chatham, NY 12136

(518) 794-9100

The Shaker Museum displays tools and machinery, furniture, oval boxes, buckets, baskets, and stoves. Represented in the collection are all the major Shaker industries, including broom making, chair making, cloak making, and the production of garden seeds and pharmaceuticals. The Shaker Museum and Library strives to provide as complete a picture of Shaker life from as great a number of Shaker communities as possible.

The Shaker Museum at South Union

PO Box 30

South Union, KY 42283

(800) 811-8379 or (502) 542-4167

Founded in 1807, the South Union community had more than three hundred members at its peak, in 1827. After the community disbanded in 1922, the buildings were sold at auction, but two original buildings were acquired by Shakertown at South Union, a nonprofit group dedicated to preserving the Shaker heritage in Kentucky. The Shaker Museum is housed in the Center Family Dwelling, and features original Shaker furniture, crafts, and textiles. Four buildings are now open, and Shakertown at South Union sponsors special exhibits, workshops, children's programs, and other events throughout the year.

Shaker Village at Pleasant Hill

3501 Lexington Road

Harrodsburg, KY 40330

(800) 734-5611

At Pleasant Hill, thirty-three original buildings have been restored. Visitors can enjoy self-guided tours through nineteenth-century buildings such as the Center Family Dwelling, the meetinghouse, and the Farm Deacons' Shop. The grounds also include demonstration kitchen and herb gardens. Demonstrations of industries include broom making, making coopers' ware, weaving, and spinning. The Trustees' Office Inn is open for meals and also offers overnight accommodations. Two craft sales shops offer handmade Shaker reproductions.

Sabbathday Lake Shaker Museum

707 Shaker Road

New Gloucester, ME 04260

(207) 926-4597

Sabbathday Lake is the only active community of Shakers still in existence. Six of the eighteen extant buildings are open to the public, and feature exhibits that explore two hundred years of Shaker history with an emphasis on the Shakers in Maine. Guided tours are available; groups require an appointment.

Sabbathday Lake Shaker Library and Archives

In 1881, Shaker Elder Otis Sawyer undertook to collect every piece written by or about the Shakers, establishing libraries both at Sabbathday Lake and at Alfred. When the Alfred community closed and its members moved to Sabbathday Lake, they brought with them their collection of Shaker material. Today, the library and archives reside in a fireproof vault in the renovated Shaker schoolhouse at Sabbathday Lake. A full-time librarian/archivist maintains the collection. Tours are offered; researchers may access the Museum collection by appointment only.

WHERE TO FIND FURNISHINGS AND ACCESSORIES IN THE SHAKER STYLE

Delnero Fine Furniture
538 Phillip Road
Fort Plain, New York 13339
(413) 527-0828
delnero.com

Delnero Fine Furniture is a small family owned and operated business that specializes in handmade furniture, including many in Shaker and early American styles. In addition, Delnero will build furniture to order, using designs provided by the customer if desired. There is a wide variety of woods to choose from, and the pieces may be custom stained in any color.

Enfield Shaker Museum Shops
2 Lower Shaker Village, NH 03748
(603) 632-4346

The Shaker village at Enfield features two on-site shops, a main shop in the Laundry/Dairy Building and another, called the Sisters' Shop, located in the Great Stone Dwelling. The shops feature an extensive selection of books, music, oval boxes, herb drying racks, Shaker Workshops furniture kits, and other Shaker-inspired gifts.

Richard Bissell Fine Woodworking
126 Signal Pine Road
Putney, VT 05346
(802) 387-4416
www.furnitureontheinternet.com
Richard Bissell offers Shaker-style furniture from chairs to beds to case pieces, and will design and build custom pieces as well. Also available are resources for amateur woodworkers, including plans, kits, and glued up panels.

Sabbathday Lake Shaker Museum Gift Shop
707 Shaker Road
New Gloucester, ME 04260
www.shaker.lib.me.us

The Shaker Museum at Sabbathday Lake stocks a unique selection of books, Shaker-made goods, locally produced handicrafts, woodenware, baskets, and a wide range of culinary herbs and medicinal teas, still packaged by the United Society of Shakers.

Shaker Furniture by Vermont Woodworkers
www.modernshakerfurniture.com

This web page highlights furnituremakers living in Vermont who work in the Shaker tradition. A link is provided to each woodworker, and the individual pages offer contact information as well as online showrooms and descriptions of the furniture.

Shaker Museum and Library Gift Shop
88 Shaker Museum Road
Old Chatham, NY 12136
www.shakermuseumandlibrary.org

The Shaker Museum and Library operates an on-site gift shop, with select pieces also available through their online retail shop. Offerings include books, crafts, herbs and teas, jewelry, music, toys, oval boxes, furniture kits, and other gift items.

The Shaker Museum at South Union Gift Shop
PO Box 30
South Union, KY 42283
www.shakermuseum.com

The Museum runs an on-site gift shop, and also operates a shop online. A large collection of reproductions is available, including baskets, oval boxes, tinware, candles, and brooms, as well as a selection of books, music, and herbs.

The Shaker Shoppe
616 Owl Hill Road
Lititz, PA 17543
(717) 626-9461
Shakershoppe.com

The Shaker Shoppe features a collection of Shaker-style furnishings, including chairs, tables, oval boxes, peg rails, wall shelves and cupboards, clocks, and more. Custom-built items are also available.

Shaker Style Furnishings
292 Chesham Road
Harrisville, NH 03450
888-824-3340
www.shakerstyle.com

Shaker Style Furnishings is committed to handmade furniture in the Shaker tradition. Their shop and online showroom feature home accents and gifts, boxes, stools and benches, chairs and rockers, occasional tables, dressers, and beds.

Shaker Workshops
The Old Schwamb Mill
18 Mill Lane
Arlington, MA
(781) 648-8809
www.shakerworkshops.com

Shaker Workshops produces fine furniture and accessories, as well as furniture kits and paints. Among the offerings are baskets, benches and settees, chairs, oval boxes, clocks, tables, cupboards, peg rails, lamps, jewelry, and books.

S. Timberlake Co.
158 Mayville Road, US Rt. 2
Bethel ME
(207) 824-6545
www.stimberlake.com

Mailing address:
PO Box 24
Bethel, ME 04217

S. Timberlake Co. makes Shaker reproduction chairs, tables, and built-to-order hardwood furniture, including desks and case pieces.

Timekeepers
1620 Squaw Court
Girard, OH 44420
(330) 545-4141
www.jolaf.com

Timekeepers creates handcrafted clocks and furniture, both Shaker reproductions and pieces in sympathy with Shaker design. All pieces are made to order.

Timothy Clark, Cabinetmaker/Chairwright
Waltham, VT
(802) 877-1058
www.timothyclark.com
Timothy Clark builds custom solid wood furniture in a style influenced by Shaker furniture traditions. Works include chairs, settees, tables, pencil post beds, and case pieces. Custom orders are welcome.

◉ FURTHER READING ◉

Many of the following books are widely available from booksellers, but some are currently out of print. These may often be found in libraries or in used book shops, including many of the fine used bookstores operating on the internet.

Abram, Norm. *Mostly Shaker from the New Yankee Workshop*. New York: Little Brown & Co., 1992.

Andrews, Edward Deming and Faith Andrews. *Shaker Furniture: The Craftsmanship of an American Communal Sect*. New York: Dover Publications, 1937.

———. *Masterpieces of Shaker Furniture*. New York: Dover Publications, 1999

Beale, Galen and Mary Rose Boswell. *The Earth Shall Blossom: Shaker Herbs and Gardening*. Woodstock, Vt.: Countryman Press, 1999.

Becksvoort, Christian and John Sheldon. *The Shaker Legacy: Perspectives on an Enduring Furniture Style*. Newtown, Conn.: Taunton Press, 1998.

Buchanan, Rita. *The Shaker Herb and Garden Book*. New York: Houghton Mifflin Co., 1996.

Burns, Deborah E. *Shaker Cities of Peace, Love, and Union: A History of the Hancock Bishopric*. Hanover, N.H.: University Press of New England, 1993.

Carr, Frances A. *Shaker Your Plate: Of Shaker Cooks and Cooking*, revised edition. United Society of Shakers, 1987.

Donaldson, Stephanie. *The Shaker Garden: Beauty through Utility*. North Pomfret, Vt.: Trafalgar Square Books, 2001.

Evelegh, Tessa. *Essential Shaker Style*. London: Ward Lock, Ltd., 1996.

Francis, Richard. *Ann the Word: The Story of Ann Lee, Female Messiah, Mother of the Shakers*. New York: Arcade Publishing, 2001.

Fuller, Persis and Amy Bess Miller. *The Best of Shaker Cooking*. New York: Macmillan Publishing, 1993.

Gillon, Edmund V. *A Cut & Assemble Shaker Village: Authentic Architectural Models in H-O Scale*. Atglen, Penn.: Schiffer Publishing, 1999.

Handberg, Ejner. *Shop Drawings of Shaker Furniture and Woodenware*. Stockbridge, Mass.: The Berkshire Traveller Press, 1973.

Horsham, Michael. *Shaker Style*. Edison, N.J.: Book Sales, Inc., 2001.

Johnson, Theordore E. and John McKee. *Hands to Work and Hearts to God: The Shaker Tradition in Maine*. Brunswick, Maine: Bowdoin College Museum of Art, 1969.

Klamkin, Marian. *Hands to Work: Shaker Folk Art and Industries*. New York: Dodd, Mead and Co., 1972.

Mahoney, Kathleen. *Wisdom from a Shaker Garden*. New York: Penguin Studio, 1998.

Meader, Robert F. *Illustrated Guide to Shaker Furniture.* New York: Dover Publications, 1972.

Miller, Amy Bess Williams. *Shaker Medicinal Herbs: A Compendium of History, Lore, and Uses.* North Adams, Mass.: Storey Books, 1999.

Morin, Frances, Catherine de Zegher, and Ann Philbin. *Heavenly Visions: Shaker Gift Drawings and Gift Songs.* Minneapolis, Minn.: University of Minnesota Press, 2002.

Morse, Flo. *The Story of the Shakers.* Woodstock, Vt.: Countryman Press, 1986.

Moser, Thomas. *How to Build Shaker Furniture,* Revised Edition. New York: Sterling Publishing Co., Inc., 1977.

Murray, Stuart. *The Shaker Heritage Guidebook: Exploring the Historic Sites, Museums, and Collections.* Spencertown, N.Y.: Golden Hill Press, 1994.

Nicoletta, Julie. *The Architecture of the Shakers.* Woodstock, Vt.: Countrymen Press, 1996.

Piercy, Caroline B. *The Shaker Cookbook: Not by Bread Alone.* New York: Random House Value Publishing, 2001.

Rieman, Timothy D. and Jean M. Burks. *The Complete Book of Shaker Furniture.* New York: Harry N. Abrams, 1993.

Rose, Milton C. and Emily Mason Rose. *Shaker Tradition and Design.* New York: Random House Value Publishers, 1983.

Sarle, Cora Helena. *A Shaker Sister's Drawings: Wild Plants Illustrated by Cora Helena Sarle.* New York: Monacelli Press, 1997.

Schreiner, Tim. *In the Shaker Style: Building Furniture Inspired by the Shaker Tradition.* Newtown, Conn.: Taunton Press, 2001.

A Shaker Gardener's Manual: Containing Plain Instructions for the Selection, Preparation, and Management of a Kitchen Garden: With Practical Directions. Bedford, Mass.: Applewood Books, 1986.

Shea, John G. *The American Shakers and Their Furniture.* New York: Van Nostrand Reinhold Co., 1971.

Shea, John G. *Making Authentic Shaker Furniture: With Measured Drawings of Museum Classics.* Dover Publications, 1992.

Sprigg, June. *Simple Gifts: Lessons in Living from a Shaker Village.* New York: Random House, 1999.

Spring, June et al. *Shaker: Life, Work, and Art.* New York: Abradale Press, 2001.

Stein, Stephen J. *The Shaker Experience in America: A History of the United Society of Believers.* Yale University Press, 1994.

Time-Life Editors. *American Style: Mission, Shaker, and Country Projects.* New York: Time Life.

Thurman, Suzanne Ruth. *O Sisters Ain't You Happy?: Gender, Family, and Community Among the Harvard and Shirley Shakers, 1781–1918* (Women and Gender in North American Religion). Syracuse, N.Y.: Syracuse University Press, 2001.

Wood, Dorothy. *Shaker.* New York: Chronicle Books, 1999.

◉ INDEX ◉

PHOTO CREDITS